PRACTICAL FISHING KNOTS

PRACTICAL FISHING KNOTS

Mark Sosin and Lefty Kreh

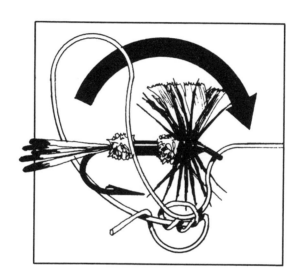

LINE DRAWINGS BY
ROD WALINCHUS

THE LYONS PRESS
GUILFORD, CONNECTICUT
AN IMPRINT OF THE GLOBE PEQUOT PRESS

Books by the Same Authors

TOGETHER

Practical Fishing Knots
Fishing the Flats
Practical Fishing Knots II

MARK SOSIN

Practical Black Bass Fishing (with Bill Dance)
Practical Light-Tackle Fishing
Through the Fish's Eye (with John Clark)
Everglades
Saltwater Fishing (with George Poveromo)
Practical Saltwater Fly Fishing

LEFTY KREH

Fly Casting with Lefty Kreh
Fly Fishing in Salt Water
Salt Water Fly Patterns
The L. L. Bean Guide to Outdoor Photography

The Lyons Press is an imprint of The Globe Pequot Press.

First Edition/Twenty-third Printing

Library of Congress Cataloging-in-Publication Data

Sosin, Mark.
   Practical fishing knots II / Mark Sosin and Lefty Kreh;
line drawings by Rod Walinchus.
     p. cm.
   Kreh's name appears first on the earlier ed.
   Rev. ed. of: Practical fishing knots. {1972}
   Includes index.
   ISBN 978-1-55821-102-5
   1. Fishing knots. I. Kreh, Lefty. II. Kreh, Lefty.
Practical fishing knots. III. Title. IV. Title: Practical fishing knots II.
V. Title: Practical fishing knots two.
SH452.9.K6K74 1991
799.1—dc20   91-7189
                       CIP

Printed in the United States of America

Contents

○

PUBLISHER'S PREFACE

○

It is just twenty years since Mark Sosin and Lefty Kreh wrote the first edition of *Practical Fishing Knots*. I remember well the long lunch we all had, when this book was first conceived, in a restaurant now replaced by a high-rise apartment building on the corner of Twenty-seventh Street and Park Avenue South in New York City. The publishing house I then worked for wrongly considered the book too narrow. Mark, Lefty, and I thought otherwise. Knots were the one common denominator that linked all brands of fishermen—from deepsea to shallow spring creek. Knots, too, led to success or heart-stopping failure.

As the 1980s wound down, I resisted the periodic comments the two increasingly busy men made about the need for a new edition: it's hard to put a book out of print that is selling better than it ever had in the past. (Sales were by then in excess of 100,000 copies.) But Mark and Lefty insisted. It was a disservice to keep the first edition in print; there were new knots, new materials, and new ways to tie old knots. Some of the old standbys just weren't needed any more. And all the knots could best be illustrated by thoughtful line drawings done by one person. The entire book could be streamlined and made more genuinely helpful.

In the end they won—as wise authors should—and the result is this handsome new edition, graced by the extremely helpful line drawings of Rod Walinchus.

We all hope it will serve the next two decades of serious fishermen as well as its predecessor served for the past twenty years.

—Nɪᴄᴋ Lʏᴏɴs

PRACTICAL FISHING KNOTS

Conversion Chart: Imperial to Metric

Imperial	Metric
Linear Measurement	

¼ inch	0.6 cm
½ inch	1.25 cm
1 inch	2.54 cm
2 inches	5.08 cm
4 inches	10.16 cm
6 inches	15.24 cm
8 inches	20.32 cm
10 inches	25.40 cm
12 inches (1 foot)	30.48 cm
2 feet	0.61 m
3 feet (1 yard)	0.91 m
5 feet	1.52 m
10 feet	3.05 m

Measures of Weight

1 lb	450 g
2 lb	900 g
5 lb	2¼ kg
10 lb	4½ kg
20 lb	9 kg
50 lb	23 kg
100 lb	46 kg

1

Understanding Knots

O

A knot is nothing more than a connection. It can be a connection in the line itself, between two lines, a joining of line and leader, or for attaching a lure, hook, swivel, or sinker. Knots have very specific uses; none suit every situation. The key lies in knowing what knot to use and when to use it.

Think of knots as links in a chain that connect you to the fish at the other end of the line. All of us know that the weakest link fails first. Choosing the right connection and tying it correctly makes that chain stronger. The ultimate goal of serious anglers focuses on maximizing tackle performance. Knots become an integral and vital part of the system.

Knot Basics

Regardless of the material, any knot begins to slip just before it breaks. The tighter you can draw a knot when tying it, the more force it can withstand before slippage occurs. A knot's effectiveness is expressed as a percentage of the line's unknotted line strength with the maximum rated at 100 percent. Most knots exceed 90 percent of the line strength on a straight pull when tied properly and drawn down as tightly as possible.

Lubricating a knot by dipping it in water or moistening it with saliva prior to drawing it down will help to seat it smoothly with a minimum of friction. With heavier lines, you must use a tool such as a pair of pliers for the final draw down. Extensive tests show that it is virtually impossible to achieve maximum tightness with bare hands. Some people insist on adding silicone or another slippery lubricant to help seat a knot. Remember that the additive remains and often increases the risk of slippage when a load is applied.

If you attempt to burn or heat the tag end of monofilament to create a burr, you could easily damage both the knot and the line. Tying an Overhand Knot in the tag end to stop slippage usually falls short and indicates that you're not seating the connection correctly.

Follow the Directions Carefully

The only place to learn to tie a specific knot is in the relaxed atmosphere ashore. Mastering anything takes practice. That's why we recommend that you tie a knot several times before adding it to your list. You have to be able to tie it quickly and comfortably.

Recognize that not everyone can tie *all* knots well. Most of us rely on two or three knots from each category to cover most situations. Once you develop a system that works for you, stick with it.

The directions for all of the knots in this book along with the accompanying illustrations are precise. If the instructions tell you to go *over* first and then *under*, follow them. Don't reverse the procedure thinking it won't make a difference. A Surgeon's Knot or Loop, for example, must have all four ends drawn at the same time or the knot will lose strength.

Pay attention to the recommended number of turns. For lines testing from 8X to six pounds, the Improved Clinch Knot should have five turns around the standing part of the main line. Four turns aren't enough to keep the knot from slipping and six turns prevent you from drawing up the knot securely.

More Facts

The finer the diameter of monofilament, the easier it is to seat the knot securely. Diameter may also be a limiting factor when selecting a knot. Some excellent knots work well with fine-diameter line, but prove useless in heavier mono because they cannot be drawn tight.

When joining two lines of equal or unequal diameter, you'll tie a better knot if both monofilaments are the same brand from the same manufacturer. Dissimilar monofilament differs in stiffness, making it more difficult to draw the knot tight.

If you want to compare different knots and don't have a line-testing machine, try this test. Tie each knot in a separate length of line or to two identical hooks. Have a friend hold both hooks or one end of each line with a pair of pliers. Use a pair of gloves to protect your hands and pull evenly on the other end. You'll quickly learn which knot is stronger.

While you're running this test, try jerking the lines. Some knots are very strong under a steady pull, but fail under impact. The Spider Hitch serves as a well-known example.

When you select knots, recognize that some take longer to tie than others. The more time-consuming connections may be a little stronger and worth the effort when you're not trying to re-rig tackle while watching a school of fish on the surface. For those situations, you should know a few knots that can be tied very quickly and still do a satisfactory job.

For the Fly Fisherman

Newcomers to fly fishing often feel overwhelmed by the choice of knots and what they perceive to be the complexities of building a leader. With only nine knots, you should be able to handle almost any fly-fishing assignment from trout to tarpon and bass to bonefish. Those knots include the Speedy Nail Knot, Whipped Loop, Surgeon's Knot, Huffnagle Knot, Bimini Twist, Non-Slip Mono Loop, Trilene Knot, George Harvey Dry-Fly Knot, and Figure-8 Knot.

Trimming a Knot

Once you seat a knot properly, it can be trimmed closely, because it won't slip. Use a pair of nail clippers, scissors, cutting pliers, or other tools made for the task. Don't try to burn the tag end, because you will weaken the knot.

Trim the knot close to the tie so that the tag end does not protrude or extend. If it does, it could catch on a guide or tiptop or it might pick up weeds. When a tag end should be left a little longer, we will indicate that in the instructions. Otherwise, trim the tag end at a 45-degree angle facing back toward the knot.

When a knot must pass back and forth through the guides while fighting a fish (particularly in fly fishing), coat the knot with a rubber-based cement that remains flexible. Epoxy is much too rigid when it hardens. The coating protects the knot so that it does not nick or catch on a guide.

Terminology

To facilitate understanding the step-by-step tying instructions for each knot, it is important that you become familiar with the following terms and their definitions:

TAG END The part of the line in which the knot is tied. Think of it as the **short** end of the line. Tag end will also be used to denote the short excess line that remains after a knot is tied. This would normally be the portion that is trimmed.

STANDING PART The main part of the line as distinguished from the tag end. This would be the line that goes to the reel or the longer end if you are working with leader material.

TURNS OR WRAPS Consider a turn or wrap to be one complete revolution of one line around another. It is usually achieved by passing the tag end around the standing part or a standing loop.

LOOP Technically, a loop is a closed curve of line. It can be formed by bringing the tag end back and alongside the standing part or by tying a knot that creates a loop.

DOUBLE LINE A double line is similar to a loop except that both strands of line are used together instead of working with the loop that is formed. If you were to pinch the round end of a loop shut with your fingers, you would create a double line. A double line is also created with certain knots, such as the Bimini Twist.

2

Knots You Should Know

○

Overhand Knot

By itself, the Overhand Knot is the weakest and poorest knot you can tie. In several more sophisticated knots, it becomes one of the steps, and that's why we are including it. Fly fishermen know it as a Wind Knot (caused by improper casting).

STEP 1 Hold the standing part of the line between the thumb and forefinger of the left hand about eight inches from the end. With the tag end between the thumb and forefinger of the right hand, rotate your right hand and bring it toward your left hand. A loop will form against the standing part of the line.

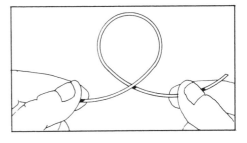

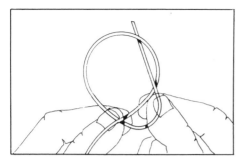

STEP 2 Slide the loop formed in **Step 1** under the thumb and forefinger of your left hand, holding it firmly. With your right hand, pass the tag end over the standing part and slip it through the loop.

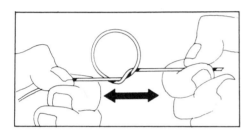

STEP 3 Moisten the knot and pull both hands apart steadily to tighten.

Bimini Twist

The Bimini Twist can be tied in monofilament or braided line, creating 100 percent knot strength. Unless you are in a fishing situation that dictates no leader and a very delicate presentation, the Bimini Twist should automatically be tied in the tag end of the line. It creates a double line with a loop and forms the heart of other connection systems.

When you put a Bimini Twist at the end of the line, any other knot you tie with the tag end (regardless of breaking strength) will not fail. Although developed for big-game trolling, the Bimini ranks as the single most important knot for light tackle and fly fishing. Once mastered, the Bimini Twist can be tied in less than thirty seconds.

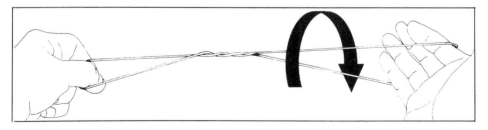

STEP 1 Measure about four feet of line (you can use more or less line depending on the size loop desired) and double the tag end back against the standing part. Grasp the standing part and the tag end between the thumb and forefinger of your left hand. Slip your right hand through the loop and against the closed end. Rotate your right hand in a clockwise direction twenty times, putting twenty twists in the line while holding the line in your left hand securely.

STEP 2 Continue to maintain pressure by holding the line securely in your left hand and pushing the back of your right hand against the closed end of the loop. Don't let the twists unwind. Bend your right knee by putting your foot on any raised object. Drape the loop over your knee. Keep the standing part of the line in your left hand and hold the tag end in your right hand. Pull toward you with both hands simultaneously and start to separate your hands. The angle at which the standing part and tag end touch the twists should **never exceed 90 degrees** (45 degrees on each side of the centerline).

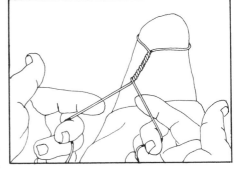

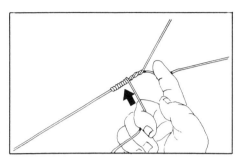

STEP 3 The key to this step lies in constantly maintaining a 90-degree angle between the standing part and the tag end. With the twists jammed together (**Step 2**), move your hands to the right (at the same time). That brings the standing part directly in line with the twists and the tag end at a right angle. Pull toward you on the standing part and ease your right hand away from you slightly until the tag end jumps the first twist. As you pull on the standing part, you have to feed the tag end gradually toward the twists. Place the forefinger of your right hand against one leg of the loop and pull toward you to continue the spiral wraps.

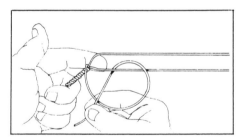

STEP 4 Don't relax the pressure on the standing part for an instant. Slide your left hand down the standing part until you can reach the final spiral wrap with the thumb and forefinger. The loop remains over your knee. As you hold the spiral wraps between the thumb and forefinger of the left hand, use your right hand to pass the tag end around the closer leg of the loop and then back through the small loop you just created. Pull the tag end toward you until the small

loop closes and then work it back toward the spiral wraps until it locks. Now you can let go with both hands and take the main loop off your knee.

STEP 5 Hold the two legs of the loop together. About two inches to the right of the twists and spiral wraps, pass the tag end over both legs of the loop and back through the small loop created by the belly in the tag end. Do the same thing four more times, working from right to left and back toward the twists.

STEP 6 Pull the tag end toward you with your left hand as you carefully work the new spirals back toward the twist. It's a process of spreading them, pulling on the tag end, spreading, and so forth until this lock knot seats tightly against the Bimini Twist. On lines heavier than twelve-pound test, grip the tag end with a pair of pliers after hand-tightening to add a final touch.

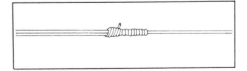

STEP 7 Trim the tag end close to the knot and the result should look like this.

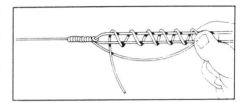

Australian Plait or Braid

Considered by some experienced skippers to be superior to the Bimini Twist, the Australian Plait or Braid takes a little longer to tie. Although both knots test at 100 percent, those who use the Australian Plait claim that the braid creates a cushioning effect. Once the knot has been built, it forms a loop (like the Bimini) and can be used in all of the applications that call for a Bimini Twist.

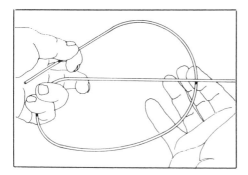

STEP 1 The standing part of the line must remain tight until the knot is completed. Leave a tag end of eighteen to twenty-four inches. The size of the loop can be adjusted as required. Start by holding the bottom of the loop (or the two legs for a longer loop) in the ring and small fingers of the left hand. The tag end is gripped with the thumb and forefinger of the left hand. Note that the tag end is **behind** the standing part. Hold the tag end and standing part at the point where they cross with the thumb and forefinger of the right hand.

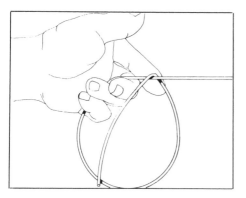

STEP 2 Cross the standing part with the tag end and bring the tag end through the loop. Continue to hold the spot where the lines cross.

STEP 3 Make a second pass over the standing part with the tag end and pass it through the loop.

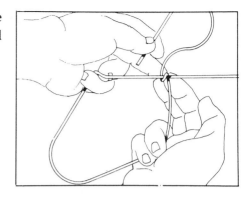

STEP 4 Check your progress. You're holding the loop (or the legs of the loop) in one hand and the tag end in the other. There are two twists created by the tag end passing around the standing part.

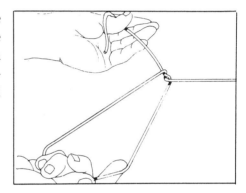

STEP 5 Pull the tag end back toward the main standing part to roll the twists in **Step 3** until they lock. Use your right hand to hold this juncture.

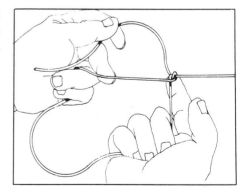

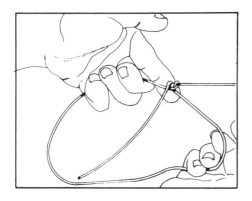

STEP 6 Continue to hold the juncture of the standing part and tag end. Pass the tag end over the top leg of the loop and down through the loop.

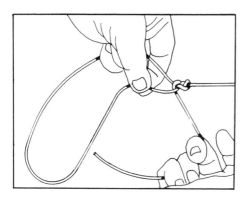

STEP 7 Pull the tag end back against the beginning of the braid and lock it in place. Then pass the standing part over the other leg of the loop and pull back on the standing part to lock it against the braid. Continue this process fifteen to twenty times on each side, alternating over one leg and then the other. It's a simple braiding process of over, under, over, under with each braid locked in place before the next one is started.

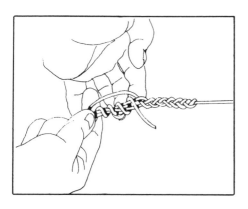

STEP 8 When you have completed the required number of braids, finish it off the same way you did with the Bimini Twist. Hold the legs of the loop together, pass the tag end over the legs about two inches from the braid, and back through the small loop that forms. Working toward the braid, make at least four more passes and

then draw the lock knot tight by working it carefully. Remember to use pliers for the final seating.

STEP 9 Trim the tag end and your finished effort should match the illustration.

STEP 10 The Australian Plait has a variety of uses where a double line is needed, including interlocking loops.

Tying to a Hook or Connector

Improved Clinch Knot

The Improved Clinch Knot ranks high on the popularity list for tying a line or leader to a hook, swivel, or lure, although its breaking strength falls in the 95-percent category. Quick and easy to tie, it works best in lines testing twelve pounds or less. Drawing the knot tight with heavier lines poses a problem. With very light mono, double the line first. If you are using heavier mono, try 3½ turns.

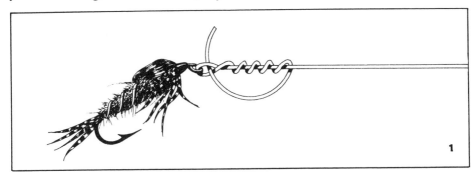

STEP 1 Insert about six inches of the tag end through the eye of the hook, bringing it back along the standing part. Make five turns with the tag end around the standing part (you may only need four turns with lines testing above 8 or 10 pounds). Then, push the tag end through the small loop at the hook eye.

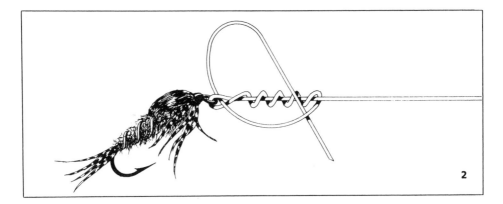

STEP 2 After passing the tag end through the first small loop, slip it through the large loose loop formed when the tag end enters the first small loop.

STEP 3 Lubricate the knot with water or saliva and pull on both the hook and the standing part of the line to draw it tight. Trim the tag end close to the knot.

Trilene Knot

A variation of the Clinch Knot, the Trilene Knot is easy to tie and stronger. Drawing it tight can be a chore in lines testing above twelve pounds. This knot is difficult to tie with very small hooks (size 18 and smaller) because the line has to be threaded through the eye twice.

STEP 1 Insert about six inches of the tag end through the eye of the hook and then pass it through a second time, forming a double loop about the size of a dime (one-half inch in diameter). The smaller these loops, the easier the knot will be to draw down. Hold the loops with the thumb and forefinger of your left hand after adjusting them to the proper size.

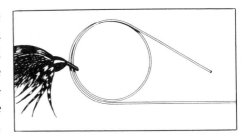

STEP 2 Holding the loops in your left hand, make five turns with the tag end around the standing part (four turns with lines ten pounds or over). Bring the tag end through both loops (created in **Step 1**). **Do not** go back through the new loop as you would in the Improved Clinch Knot.

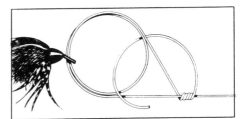

STEP 3 Moisten the knot. It will draw down better if you pull on the tag end as well as the standing part. You may have to use your teeth for the tag end, or alternate pulls. Be sure to seat this knot as tightly as possible before trimming the tag end.

Palomar Knot

The Palomar Knot comes close to 100-percent efficiency when tied properly, but you have to use more line to tie it. If you use it in a tapered leader (fly fishing), it shortens the leader more quickly than other knots. Many anglers don't use this knot with lures that have treble hooks, because you have to pass the lure through the line. It proves fast and easy, though, with a single hook or swivel.

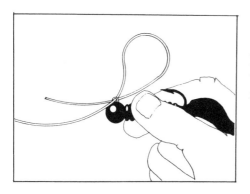

STEP 1 Double four to six inches of the tag end back along the standing part, forming a loop. Pass this loop through the eye of the hook or the ring of the swivel.

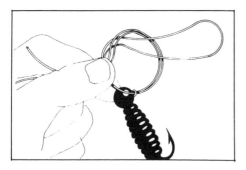

STEP 2 Make an Overhand Knot with the loop, as shown.

STEP 3 Slip the hook, swivel, or lure through the loop. At the same time, hold the tag end and standing part together in your left hand and pull slowly until the loop clears the lure, hook, or swivel. Moistening the knot helps.

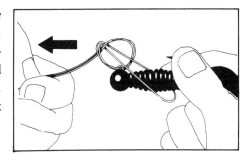

STEP 4 Continue pulling the tag end and standing part while holding the lure, hook, or swivel in your right hand until the knot seats securely. Trim the tag end and you're finished.

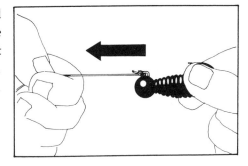

Jansik Special

The Jansik Special has our vote for tying a single strand of light monofilament to a hook, swivel, or lure, checking out very close to 100 percent. Use it with lines testing up to seventeen or twenty pounds. You'll have to practice drawing it up, because you have to pull in three directions at the same time. Holding the tag end in your teeth will help.

STEP 1 Start with a tag end at least a foot long and pass it through the hook eye two times and three times around the two coils. Practice will make it easier to determine the exact length of the tag end you will need.

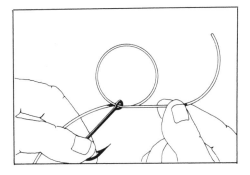

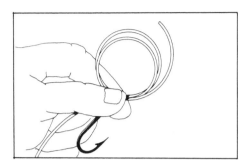

STEP 2 Work the loops until they are the same size (one-half to three-quarters inch in diameter) and pinch all three together at the hook eye with the thumb and forefinger of your left hand.

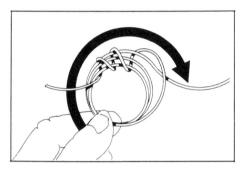

STEP 3 Bring the tag end around again as if you were going through the hook eye a fourth time. Instead, pass the tag end around all three coils three times, being careful to hold the coils together.

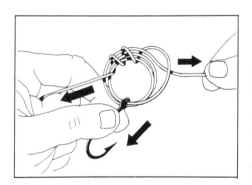

STEP 4 Moisten the knot well. Hold the hook in your left fingers, the standing part of the line in your right hand, and use your teeth to grip the tag end. You can pull both the hook and tag end with the left hand if you desire. Work the knot slowly to tighten, allowing each strand and coil to seat uniformly. It takes a little practice to juggle the three ends, but the finished product is worth the effort. Trim the tag end when the knot is secure.

Snelling a Hook

The Snell proves to be an exceptionally strong connection for attaching a leader to a hook, although many anglers ignore this important option. Tied properly and seated securely, it usually will test at 100 percent. Here's one way to do it.

STEP 1 You'll need at least a foot of tag end to snell. Insert the tag end through the eye of the hook and pull it through toward the bend of the hook. Make a large loop with the tag end and insert it back through the hook eye in the same direction, allowing it to lie along the hook shank.

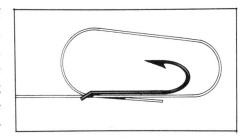

STEP 2 Hold the eye of the hook and the leader with your left hand. Insert two fingers of your right hand in the loop formed in **Step 1** and rotate the loop around the hook shank at least six times. You are making the wraps from the hook eye back toward the point.

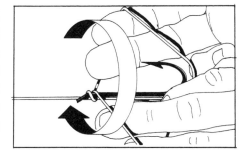

STEP 3 Grasp the last wrap with the thumb and forefinger of your right hand to prevent any unraveling. Pull on the standing part slowly to draw the remaining loop under the wraps. When the snell is semi-tight, slide the

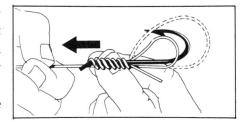

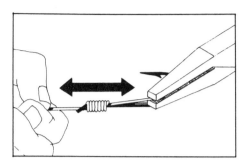

wraps along the hook shank until they shoulder the hook eye. Then, grip the tag end with pliers and pull on both the tag end and standing part at the same time. This will seat the knot. Trim the tag end.

Crawford Knot

The Crawford Knot can be tied exceptionally fast and is often used when one has to change a lure or fly in a hurry. It's not a particularly strong knot compared to others, and seldom tests more than 90 percent.

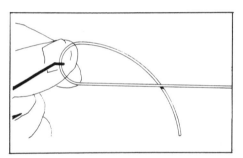

STEP 1 Hold the hook in your left hand. Insert about six inches of the tag end through the eye of the hook and grasp both the tag end and standing part at the hook eye with the thumb and forefinger of your left hand.

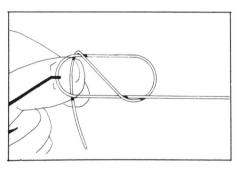

STEP 2 Pass the tag end behind and around the standing part to form an oval loop. Working back toward the eye of the hook, lay the tag end on a diagonal across both legs of the loop and pass it behind the loop.

STEP 3 Reverse direction with the tag end and lay it across the front of the loop to form a figure eight. Continue holding the strands with the thumb and forefinger of your left hand.

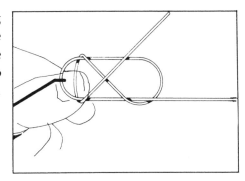

STEP 4 Pass the tag end over the top strand of the loop and then feed it back through the top of the loop as shown. Moisten the knot and pull firmly on the tag end until the loop closes.

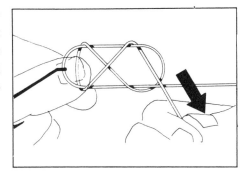

STEP 5 Finish the knot by pulling on both the hook and the standing part at the same time. When the knot is seated, tug on the standing part two or three times to make sure the knot won't slip. Then trim the tag end.

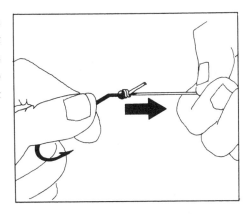

Offshore Swivel Knot

Designed originally to attach a swivel to a double line for offshore big-game fishing, the Swivel Knot can also be used for attaching a hook. It has excellent applications when fishing natural bait in shallow water for species such as bonefish or permit when a leader isn't used. The Swivel Knot proves exceptionally strong. If one strand breaks, the other probably will hold regardless of the amount of stress on the knot. You should put a Bimini Twist in the line first.

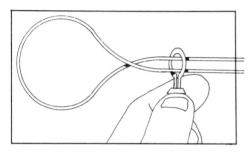

STEP 1 Insert the loop from a Bimini Twist or Australian Plait through the ring of the swivel (or hook eye) and make one twist.

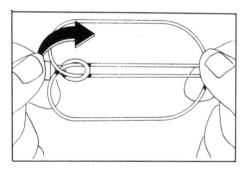

STEP 2 Lay the tag end of the loop back against the standing part of the loop, being careful to keep the one twist in it. Pinch the round end of the loop against the standing part with your thumb and forefinger.

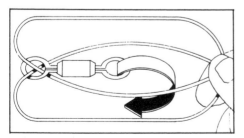

STEP 3 Swing the swivel through **both** loops six times. Continue to hold the loop end and the standing part together so that the knot will not unravel.

STEP 4 Particularly with heavy line, tightening the knot takes time. Hold the swivel in one hand (use pliers if necessary) and both strands of the standing part in the other. Moisten the knot thoroughly. Pull on the swivel to slide the knot down. You probably will have to alternate between pulling and pushing the twists together. Make sure all of the twists seat tightly against the swivel ring.

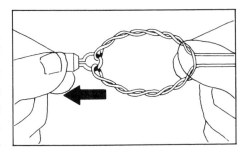

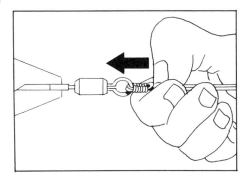

Arbor Knot

Several knots serve the purpose of securing the end of the line to the arbor of a reel, but this one is easy to tie and does the job well. It's strong enough to hold if a rod and reel go overboard and you have to pull them up by the line.

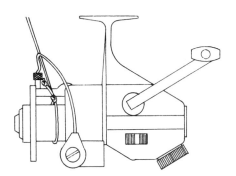

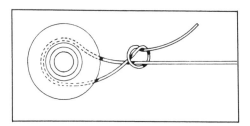

STEP 1 Circle the arbor of the spool with the tag end of the line. Then, tie an Overhand Knot around the standing part.

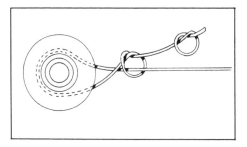

STEP 2 Tie a second Overhand Knot in the tag end no more than two or three inches from the first Overhand Knot.

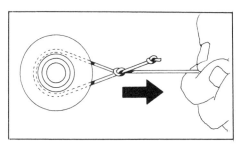

STEP 3 Moisten the line and the two Overhand Knots. Hold the reel or spool in your left hand and pull on the standing part of the line with your right hand. The first Overhand Knot will slide down to the arbor and the second Overhand Knot will serve as a jam. Trim the tag end so that it doesn't catch line stored on the spool.

Tandem-Hook Rig

The Tandem-Hook Rig represents an easy way to add a second hook in line with the first. It is particularly effective for including a tail hook.

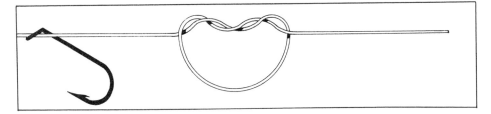

STEP 1 Insert the tag end through the eye of the first hook and leave a considerable amount of excess for tying the second hook. Then make a Double Overhand Knot (pass the tag end through the loop twice).

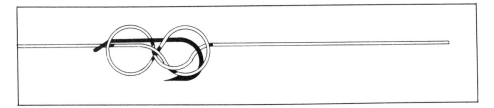

STEP 2 Pull gently on the standing part and tag end until the Double Overhand Knot "turns over," forming a figure-eight. After figure eight is formed push on both line ends to enlarge the figure eight. Pass the hook through both loops of the figure eight and continue to tighten slowly until the knot seats at the eye of the first hook.

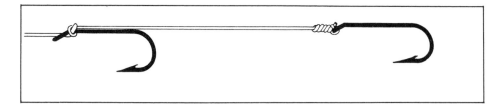

STEP 3 When the Figure-Eight Knot has been seated, tie on the second hook using any of the basic connection knots. Be sure to adjust the distance of the second hook so that it fits the bait you plan to use.

3

Joining Lines Together

O

Joining two lines together involves one of the most important applications of knot building. Construction weakness undermines the entire tackle system and handicaps the angler. The most obvious application lies in attaching a heavier leader to the line. That leader may be monofilament or a dissimilar material such as braided wire or single-strand. Even if you intend to tie mono to mono, differences exist in stiffness and other properties.

You will also encounter situations where you have to tie together two sections of the same line. If you troll with wire line such as Monel, it has to be joined to monofilament or Dacron.

A number of knots do a satisfactory job of joining two lines, but as you review this section, you'll discover that some are more specialized than others and tailored for specific assignments. We recommend that you try several knots and eventually settle on two or three that work well for you.

Surgeon's Knot

Physicians tell us that they have never seen this knot used in a surgical procedure, so the origin of its name remains a mystery. It still ranks as one of the best and fastest knots for joining lines of equal or unequal diameters and similar or dissimilar materials. The Surgeon's Knot should not be used if one strand of monofilament exceeds sixty-pound test, because it cannot be drawn tight with hand pressure.

If you use it to join mono to braided wire, the monofilament should test between twelve and forty pounds, while the braided wire should not exceed forty pounds.

When you analyze the Surgeon's Knot, it's nothing more than a Double Overhand Knot utilizing both strands. Some people report that they have had trouble learning it from drawings. We believe it's because they fail to recognize that the leader (shown in black) is short enough to pass the end through the loop.

Properly constructed, the Surgeon's Knot approaches 100-percent efficiency and can be tied in the dark. It's that easy. Just remember that when you tighten the knot, you must pull on all four strands.

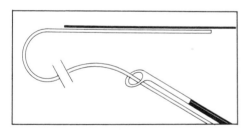

STEP 1 The line from the reel or the loop of the Bimini Twist extends from left to right and the tag end of the leader extends from right to left. Lay the line and the leader side by side for at least twelve inches.

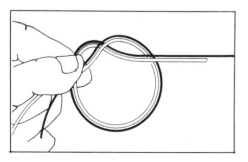

STEP 2 Pinch the two lines together with the thumb and forefinger of your left hand. Use your right hand to make an Overhand Knot (as shown) with both the line and the leader. Keep the loop open.

STEP 3 Pass the line and leader through the loop again, making a Double Overhand Knot. You are simply repeating **Step 2** again.

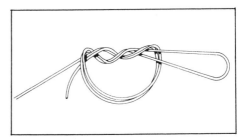

STEP 4 Hold the standing part of the line and the tag end of the leader together in your left hand. Grasp the tag end of the line and the standing part of the leader in your right hand. **You must keep line and leader together when tightening the knot.** Moisten the knot thoroughly prior to tightening. Pull all four ends **at the same time** as tightly as possible.

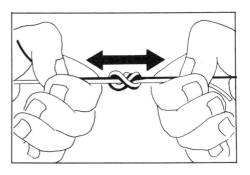

STEP 5 Before you trim the knot, pull the individual strands to make sure the knot is drawn up fully.

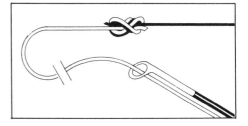

Simple Blood Knot

The conventional Blood Knot has been a favorite with fly fishermen for decades and is often used to join lines in other fishing situations. We call this modification the Simple Blood Knot. It's easier to tie and comes close to 100-percent efficiency, based on our line testers and fishing experiences.

We caution you to follow the recommended number of turns precisely. You should also know that this knot is difficult to seat if one of the lines breaks in excess of twenty-pound test.

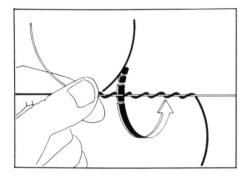

STEP 1 We have determined that maximum strength occurs when you make **seven** turns with each line. Cross the tag ends of the two lines to be joined, leaving six to eight inches extending on each tag end. Grasp the two lines at the point where they cross with the thumb and forefinger of your left hand. Use your right hand to wrap the tag end of the line crossing from the left around the standing part of the line on the right exactly seven times. Work from left to right.

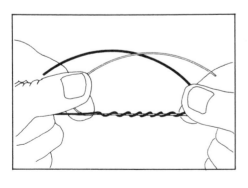

STEP 2 Fold the tag end that you just wrapped **behind** the tag end on the left as shown. Change your grip so that you can pinch the two lines together with the fingers of your left hand at the spot where they cross. Notice that a loop has been formed. Use your right hand to make seven wraps with the second tag end

around the first tag end, passing it through the loop on each wrap. Remember that you always wrap from left to right.

STEP 3 When you have finished all the wraps, the knot looks like the drawing. Moisten the knot. Start pulling slowly on both tag ends to close the knot. Then, pull slowly on the two standing parts. **Alternate this process (tag ends, standing parts, tag ends, standing parts) until the knot seats firmly.**

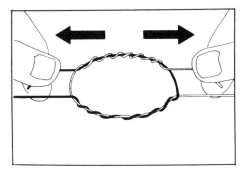

STEP 4 Note that the tag ends oppose each other at opposite ends of the knot when it is tied correctly. If you achieve this, the knot should approximate 100-percent efficiency. Trim the tag ends and the lines have been joined.

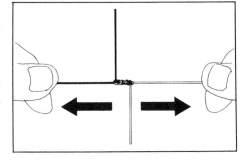

Huffnagle Knot

Designed to join a light fly leader tippet to very heavy monofilament (80- to 120-pound test), the Huffnagle Knot enables the angler to achieve a small connection that lies straight. Several variations of the knot are currently being used, but the method illustrated works as well as any. Start by tying a Bimini Twist in the end of the lighter line.

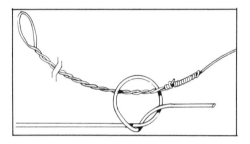

STEP 1 Make an Overhand Knot in the heavy shock leader and pass the loop of the Bimini Twist through the open Overhand Knot.

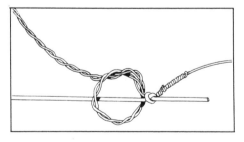

STEP 2 Grasp the tag end of the shock leader with pliers and grip the standing part of the leader with the left hand. Seat the Overhand Knot as tightly as possible, making sure that the Bimini Twist rests right against it. Trim the tag end of the heavy shock leader.

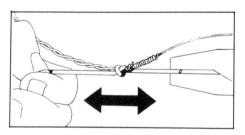

STEP 3 Tie an Overhand Knot with the double line from the Bimini Twist around the standing part of the shock leader. Tease the Overhand Knot closed, working it back against the Overhand Knot in the shock leader.

STEP 4 Finish the knot the same way you would secure a Bimini Twist. Make a loop with the tag end and wrap the tag end back toward the overhand knot.

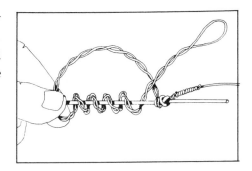

STEP 5 Moisten the loose wraps. Hold the standing part of the shock leader in your left hand and the tag end of the Bimini Twist in your right hand. Pull on the tag end until the wraps seat tightly against the Overhand Knot.

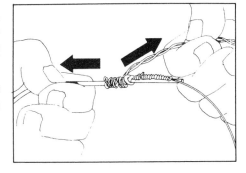

STEP 6 Trim the tag end of the light line, and the Huffnagle Knot is finished.

Albright Knot with a Lock

The Albright Knot should be in everyone's arsenal. It represents one of the most reliable connections for joining lines of greatly unequal diameters or different materials (including mono to braided or single-strand wire). It's bulkier than the Huffnagle and is slightly offset, but it's easy to tie and worth learning. We've been using a simple lock on this knot for years to prevent it from failing when fighting a big fish. That trick came from a guide at Casa Mar, a well-known tarpon camp in Costa Rica.

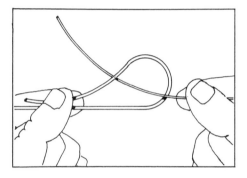

STEP 1 Bend a loop in the tag end of the heavier monofilament or braided wire and hold it with the thumb and forefinger of your left hand. If the heavier material is single-strand wire, put a Haywire Twist in the wire or bend it with pliers to create a tight loop. Insert the tag end of the lighter line (which is usually a Bimini Twist) through the loop so that the tag end rises above the loop. Allow at least eight to ten inches.

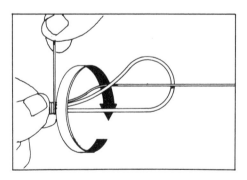

STEP 2 Slip the tag end of the lighter line under your left thumb and pinch it against the two strands of the loop. You're about to make a series of wraps with the tag end around all three strands working from left to right. The trick lies in moving your left hand to cover the wraps as they accumulate without releasing the pressure. The first wrap with the tag end must reverse direction from left to right. Try to lay each wrap shouldering the one before it. With a Bimini

Twist, ten wraps are sufficient, but you'll need at least twelve wraps with a single line.

STEP 3 After completing the wraps, insert the tag end of the lighter line back through the loop so that it exits on the same side of the loop it entered. Pull gently on the standing part to jam the wraps together, holding the wraps lightly between left thumb and forefinger, and start sliding them toward the closed end of the loop.

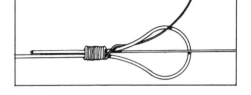

STEP 4 Hold the standing part of the heavier leader in your left hand and push the wraps with the thumb and forefinger as you pull on the standing part of the light line. Work slowly so you don't slide the wraps over the end. Alternate pulling on the tag end of the lighter line and the standing part until the wraps are jammed against the tag end. Then, use pliers to pull the tag end even tighter.

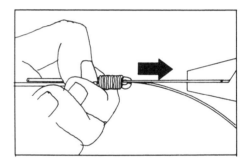

STEP 5 Finally, pull on the standing parts of both lines to make sure the knot is seated securely.

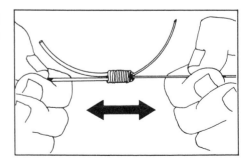

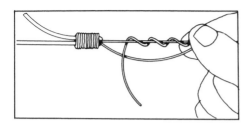

STEP 6 To lock the knot so the tag end cannot slip out, loop the tag end back toward the heavier leader and make three wraps around the lighter leader (just as you would finish a Bimini Twist).

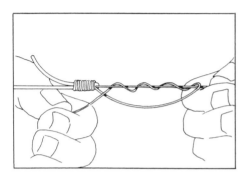

STEP 7 Pull on tag end to firmly secure knot. When they are on the same side as the lighter line, pull on the tag end of the lighter line to tighten them. If you want a smaller lock, work these wraps back toward the Albright before tightening.

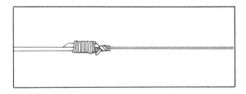

STEP 8 Trim the tag ends, and the result should look like this drawing.

Joining Monel to Braided Line

Those who troll deep with wire line face the task of joining the wire (usually Monel) to braided backing. Wire should only be spooled on a conventional reel with a core of braided line underneath to absorb the pressure.

STEP 1 Put a Bimini Twist in the end of the braided line. Insert the tag end of the wire up through the loop, leaving about eighteen inches.

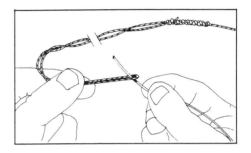

STEP 2 The next three steps are easier if you keep pressure on both the wire and the braided line. Spiral wrap the wire five to seven times around both strands of the Bimini, working from right to left.

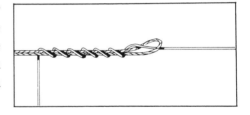

STEP 3 Reverse the direction of the spiral wraps, moving from left to right and back toward the end loop of the Bimini. These reverse wraps cross the original ones made in **Step 2**. Pass the tag end of the wire back through the loop, exiting on the same side as the one the wire entered.

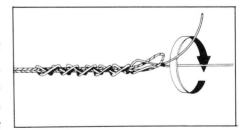

STEP 4 Finish the connection with four or five barrel wraps around the standing part of the wire. Never trim the tag end of wire by cutting it. Instead, rock the tag end back and forth until it breaks. This eliminates any burr that could cause a nasty cut in someone's hand.

4

Loops

Loops become an integral part of any leader system. Attaching one to the eye of an artificial lure gives it more action. Interlocking loops form the heart of fly-fishing leader systems and could be used for other purposes. Offshore anglers who use snap swivels hang pre-made leaders on the snap as a quick way to change bait or rigs.

When a loop is tied in heavy leader material and fished with light line, the strength of that loop lacks importance. A loop in light line or leader must be exceptionally strong to preserve the integrity of the system. Here are several options from which you can choose.

Non-Slip Loop

The Non-Slip Loop doesn't slip and often tests close to 100 percent of the unknotted line strength. It is definitely superior to the Homer Rhode Loop Knot (which should be tied in heavy leader only) and the Duncan Loop (Uni-Knot) which lacks significant strength and tightens when a big fish is hooked.

When tying this knot, the number of turns taken with the tag end around the standing part must be precise. For lines testing from 8X to six pounds, use **seven** turns; **five** turns for lines in the eight to twelve-pound class; **four** turns for fifteen to forty-pound line; **three** turns for fifty or sixty-pound; and **two** turns for lines heavier than that. This knot is also recommended for the new braided lines and you should use a minimum of **six** turns.

STEP 1 Begin the knot before you pick up the fly or lure. Make an Overhand Knot in the line and then pass the tag end through the eye of the hook or lure. Allow about twelve inches of tag end until you become proficient. Insert the tag end back through the loop in the Overhand Knot, **making certain it goes back through on the same side it came out originally** (see illustration).

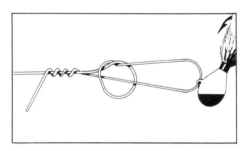

STEP 2 Wrap the tag end around the standing part the required number of times (see guide in text above).

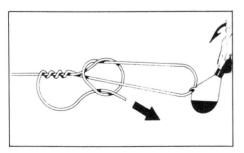

STEP 3 Insert the tag end back through the loop of the Overhand Knot. **Again, make sure it re-enters from the same side it exited** (see illustration).

STEP 4 Moisten the knot and start to seat it by pulling slowly on the tag end. This pulls the wraps together. Before the wraps are totally tight, hold the standing part of the line in your left hand and the lure or hook in your right hand. Pull your hands apart to finish tightening the knot, and trim the tag end.

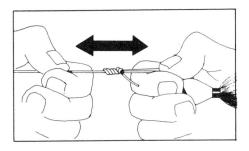

Surgeon's Loop

The Surgeon's Loop is tied exactly like the Surgeon's Knot except that it is accomplished with a single length of line. It forms one of the quickest loops, and we have used it successfully for many years.

STEP 1 Double the tag end of the line back against the standing part, leaving six to eight inches for tying the loop. Hold the tag end against the standing part with your left hand and make an Overhand Knot using both strands.

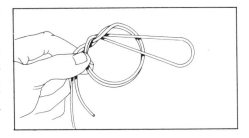

STEP 2 Make a second pass with the double line through the overhand loop to create a Double Overhand Knot.

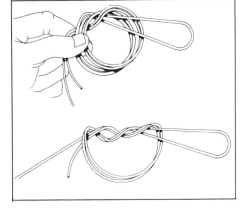

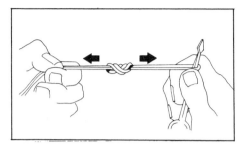

STEP 3 Moisten the knot thoroughly. Insert in the loop the handle of a pair of fishing pliers or some other object that won't nick or score the line. Grasp the tag end and standing part together in your left hand and pull your hands apart evenly until the knot is as tight as you can make it. Trim the tag end. The Surgeon's Loop tests close to 100 percent, but it becomes difficult to draw down in lines testing more than fifty or sixty pounds.

Homer Rhode Loop Knot

A favorite with many anglers for attaching a lure to a heavy leader because it can be tied quickly and easily, the Homer Rhode Loop Knot works in both monofilament and plastic-coated braided wire. It has mediocre strength and should only be used when the leader material is at least **twice** the breaking strength of the fishing line.

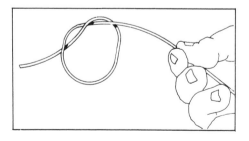

STEP 1 Before picking up the fly or lure, make an Overhand Knot in the heavy leader material, leaving a tag end of about six inches.

STEP 2 Insert the tag end through the eye of the hook or lure.

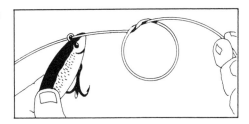

STEP 3 Pass the tag end back through the Overhand Knot, checking to insure that it re-enters on the same side it exited.

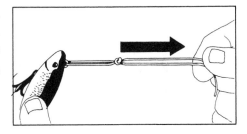

STEP 4 Hold the lure in your left hand and the tag end and standing part in your right hand. Use your fingers to pull on the standing part to tighten the Overhand Knot.

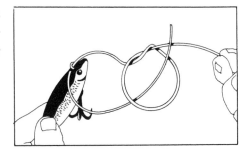

STEP 5 Pull on the tag end to slide the Overhand Knot against the eye of the lure or hook.

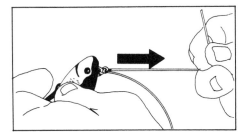

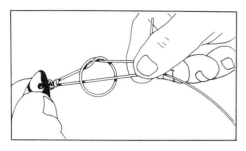

STEP 6 With the tag end, form another Overhand Knot around the standing part. Recognize that the spot on the standing part where you tighten this Overhand Knot will determine the size of the loop. Adjust the position of the Overhand Knot to create a loop of the desired size.

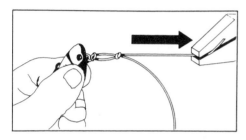

STEP 7 Use a pair of pliers to seat the second Overhand Knot by pulling on the tag end.

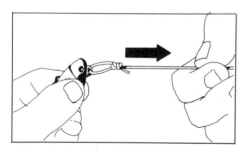

STEP 8 Pull on the standing part, and the first Overhand Knot (next to the eye of the hook or lure) will slide toward the second Overhand Knot and seat against it. That forms the loop. Trim the tag end.

Duncan Loop or Uni-Knot

Although very popular, the Duncan Loop is not particularly strong (it's basically a Clinch Knot), and the loop tends to slide under pressure. You can use it to create a loop in front of a lure or for attaching line to the arbor of a reel spool.

STEP 1 Pass the tag end of the leader through the eye of the lure or around the spool and bring it back alongside the standing part. Allow about six to eight inches to finish the knot. Hold the tag end against the standing part about six inches from the bitter end. Bend the end back toward the lure or spool, forming a loop beneath the two strands.

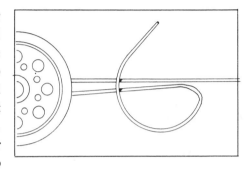

STEP 2 Starting at the end closer to the lure or spool, make four or five wraps with the tag end around both strands, passing the tag end through the loop after each wrap.

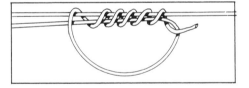

STEP 3 Pull steadily on the tag end to draw the wraps together.

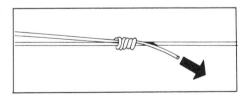

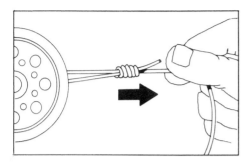

STEP 4 Moisten the knot and the loop. If you have used the knot to secure the line to the reel arbor, pull on the standing part until the knot slides right down to the hub and seats. Trim the tag end.

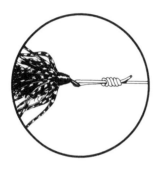

STEP 5 To form a loop in front of a fly or lure, slide the knot slowly by pulling on the standing part. When a loop of the desired size is created, use a pair of pliers to pull the tag end. The loop will remain under typical fishing conditions, but could slip down to the eye of the hook or lure when fighting a big fish. Trim the tag end.

Perfection Loop

One of the favorite knots for making an end loop, the Perfection Loop can be tied in seconds once the technique is mastered. It's strong and effective.

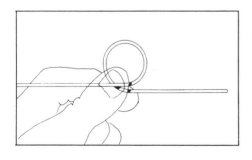

STEP 1 Hold the leader about six inches from the tag end between the thumb and forefinger of your left hand. Take the tag end in your right hand and make a loop under the standing part being held in your left hand. To do this, rotate your right wrist under your left hand. Lay the loop against the standing part by slipping it between the thumb and fore-

finger of your left hand. Hold both strands together.

STEP 2 The loop is now being held between your left thumb and forefinger. Take the tag end in your right hand and pass it over your left thumb and back behind the first loop. This creates a second loop in front of the first one. Slip the line between your left thumb and forefinger **behind** the first loop and hold all the strands together.

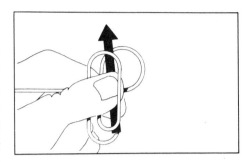

STEP 3 Take the tag end in your right hand again and lay it between the two loops with the bitter end pointing away from you. Pinch the tag end with your left thumb and forefinger to hold it in place. Reach behind and then through the first loop with the thumb and forefinger of your right hand and pull the second loop through the first.

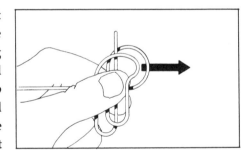

STEP 4 Continue pulling the loop with your right hand while holding the standing part in your left hand to tighten the loop. Most of us use the handle of fishing pliers or a round object to pull the loop tight. If you are making up a lot of leaders, use a nail driven in wood or a small projection to hold the loop while you pull on the standing part.

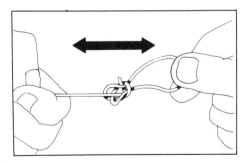

Egg Loop

Steelheaders and salmon fishermen rely on this knot to attach a cluster of eggs or yarn to a hook. The Egg Loop is really a variation of snelling a hook, but it works best with hooks that have turned-up or turned-down eyes.

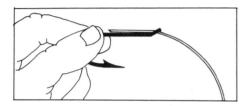

STEP 1 Insert the tag end of the leader through the eye of the hook, lay it against the shank of the hook, and hold it there with your left hand.

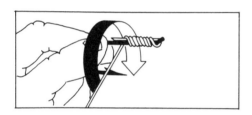

STEP 2 Bring the standing part around the eye of the hook and make five to seven wraps, working from the eye back toward the bend.

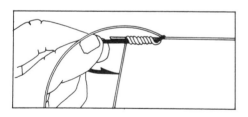

STEP 3 Hold the wraps securely with the thumb and forefinger of your left hand. Pass the other tag end of the leader through the eye of the hook, leaving a loop.

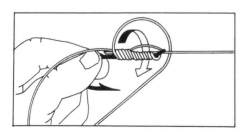

STEP 4 Change your grip so that you hold the wraps with your right hand—or turn the hook around. Take the strand of the loop closer to the eye of the hook and continue wrapping it around the hook shank five to

seven times. Hold the new wraps securely.

STEP 5 Pull the standing part of the line to eliminate the loop and draw it under the wraps. You may have to guide or untwist the loop as you pull on the standing part.

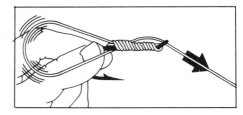

STEP 6 Trim any extension of the tag end under the wraps. The finished Egg Loop looks like the illustration.

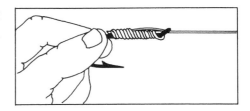

STEP 7 By pushing the standing part back through the hook eye, you open the loop on the hook, allowing you to place yarn or an egg sac under the standing part.

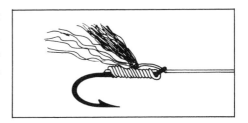

STEP 8 When you pull the standing part again, the loop closes, trapping the egg cluster, yarn, or anything else underneath it.

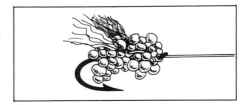

Splicing a Loop in Dacron

Dacron line is braided with a hollow core. Fly fishermen prefer it to other lines for backing on fly reels, and it also finds use on the offshore grounds with heavy tackle. Many knots designed for monofilament cannot be tied in Dacron because it won't slide easily. You can make a loop with a Bimini Twist, and this is the preferred method in twenty-pound-class Dacron. Dacron testing thirty pounds or heavier is easy to splice. The splice passes through rod guides much more smoothly than any knot.

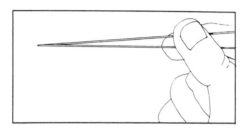

STEP 1 Cut a fourteen- to sixteen-inch length of single-strand stainless-steel trolling wire and bend it in half. The wire should be as fine diameter as possible. We recommend #2 or #3 wire.

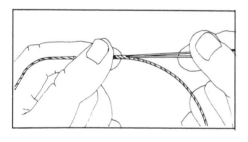

STEP 2 Before starting the splice, determine how large you want the loop to be and leave adequate tag end to create a loop of that size. The standing part of the Dacron lies to the right and the tag end to the left. Insert the wire at least twelve inches from the tag end, probing with the sharp point until you locate the hollow core. Then, work the wire through the core for a distance of four to six inches.

STEP 3 When you have pushed the wire the required distance, work it back out of the braid. Open the loop in the wire and insert the tag end of the Dacron. Be sure to put only about one-eighth inch of the tag end into the loop. The wire loop should close around the tag end the moment you release pressure.

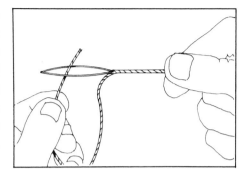

STEP 4 Hold the Dacron at the point where the wire exits (not shown), using the thumb and forefinger of your left hand. With your right hand, pull the wire back out of the Dacron. Then, continue pulling the tag end of the Dacron until the loop reaches the desired size.

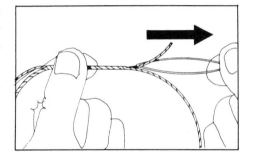

STEP 5 Slip your left hand in the loop and hold the standing part in your right hand. Pull your hands apart to tighten the splice. The braid works like the Chinese "two-finger puzzle": the more you pull, the tighter it becomes.

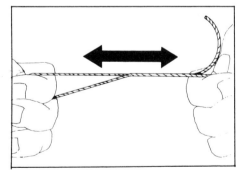

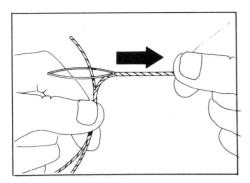

STEP 6 To prevent the loop from coming loose, repeat the procedure behind the first splice. Make sure the wire exits about one inch from the end of the first splice.

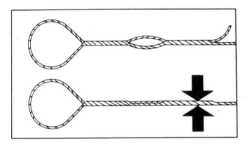

STEP 7 Before you pull on the line, determine where the tag end will exit the second splice. Trim it just short of this spot so the tag end lies **inside** the second splice. Put a light application of glue where the tag end is buried inside.

Interlocking Loops

To achieve maximum strength, loops must be interlocked correctly. Otherwise, one line will cut through the other and destroy the integrity of the system. Interlocking loops make a very strong connection when the right loops are selected.

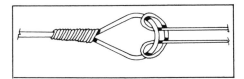

STEP 1 If a Girth Hitch is used, you sacrifice considerable strength.

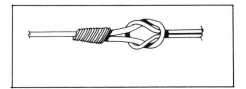

STEP 2 The loops should interlock to form a Square Knot, distributing the stress equally and evenly. This is the way an Interlocking Loop should look when tightened.

5

Wire, Cable, and Heavy Mono

○

Monofilament leaders produce more strikes than wire or cable and should be used whenever possible. Fish sometimes exhibit a shyness to wire. For those species with dentures that make a razor blade or a meat cleaver seem dull, a choice doesn't exist. If you fail to use wire or cable and aren't lucky enough to hook that critter on the outside of its jaw, the battle ends shortly after it begins. As a compromise, try using the shortest length of wire of the finest diameter compatible with the circumstances.

The bills of sailfish and marlin can be more abrasive than a coarse file, and wear through lighter monofilament if the fight lasts any length of time. Seasoned veterans opt for heavier mono leaders, particularly with huskier marlin. Seating a knot in bulky mono becomes a chore, so most regulars resort to crimped sleeves. Properly done, a crimp is amazingly strong.

Types of Wire

Single-strand stainless-steel wire is sized or gauged by a series of numbers starting with #2 and running through #19. The greater the number, the larger the diameter (and breaking strength) of the wire. An open debate continues whether or not bright wire is more visible to a fish than coffee-colored wire. We prefer the latter. Single-strand ranks at the top of the popularity list, but it does have the disadvantage of kinking and breaking if not handled carefully.

Some fishermen prefer to use braided-wire leaders because they are more supple and will not kink (although they **can** curl). Made from several strands twisted together, braided wire is available plain or nylon-coated. It is rated solely by breaking strength and does not have gauge numbers.

Big-game anglers often used forty-nine-strand aircraft cable. Such material should **never** be handled without heavy gloves when wiring a fish. Connections with this heavy cable must be made with crimped sleeves.

The Haywire Twist

The Haywire Twist is the strongest connection for attaching single-strand wire to a hook, swivel, or for making a loop in the end. It is actually a combination of a Haywire and a Barrel Twist. The Haywire segment locks the wire and keeps it from slipping.

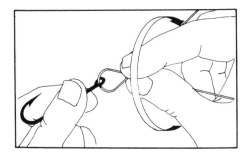

STEP 1 Insert the tag end of the wire through the eye of the hook or swivel, or simply form a small loop. Then, cross the tag end over the standing part. Hold the small loop in your left hand. Make sure the standing part and the tag end cross at an angle in excess of 90 degrees.

STEP 2 To form the Haywire, you must twist both the tag end and standing part of the wire at the same time, while holding the loop securely in the other hand. This is accomplished in half-turn increments. Done correctly, each twist forms an **X**. If you fail to maintain at least a 90-degree angle between the tag end and standing part, the tag end will merely wrap around the standing part, and you will sacrifice considerable strength. Make at least 3½ Haywire wraps before starting the Barrel wrap.

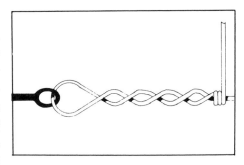

STEP 3 To start the Barrel wrap, push the tag end until it is at right angles to the standing part. Then, make several Barrel wraps, keeping each one shouldering the wrap before. Note that these wraps should be made one-half turn at a time. When you have made several Barrel wraps, bend the tag end to form a "handle" that you can grasp. Rock the handle back and forth until the wire breaks.

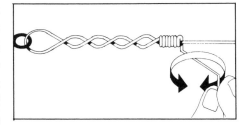

STEP 4 Never cut the tag end of the wire with pliers. It leaves a burr that can slice a hand as effectively as a razor blade. When the Haywire Twist is completed, you can run your bare hand over it and it will feel smooth.

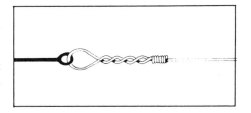

Figure-8 Knot

For those who use braided wire (either coated or uncoated), the Figure-8 Knot offers a quick and strong way to connect it to a hook or lure. Other options include the Non-Slip Mono Loop and the Homer Rhode Loop Knot.

If you leave at least one-quarter inch of the tag end extending beyond the finished Figure-8, you have the option of pushing it back through the loop and untying the knot. This allows you to change lures without cutting the wire, and you can tie on the new lure easily. The Figure-8 Knot does not work with cable.

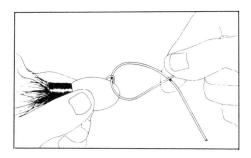

STEP 1 Insert three to five inches of the tag end through the hook eye and then pass it under the standing part to form a loop.

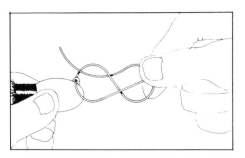

STEP 2 Pass the tag end over the standing part, forming a second loop of a figure eight. Slip the tag end back through the loop you created in **Step 1,** exactly as illustrated.

STEP 3 **To tighten the knot, pull on the tag end with a pair of pliers. Never** seat the knot by pulling on the standing part. If you do, kinks in the braided wire created during the building of the knot will be drawn into the leader and could affect the action. Trim the tag end once the knot is seated, leaving about one-quarter inch, so that you can untie it.

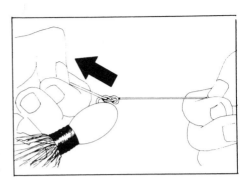

STEP 4 The top illustration shows how a kink forms in front of the hook if you pull on the standing part of the line to seat the Figure-8. The bottom drawing reflects the straight leader that occurs when you use the tag end to tighten the knot.

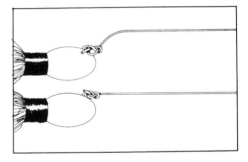

Crimping Basics

Sleeves are made in three basic shapes: round, single-barrel oval, and double-barrel oval. The double-barrel sleeve should always be used with monofilament, and works well with any material. The single-barrel oval and round sleeve should be limited to wire and cable. Oval-shaped sleeves are the better choice because of the type of crimp employed. Sleeves intended for monofilament are longer than those designed for cable.

The greater the wall thickness of the sleeve, the stronger it is; that's important when wrestling with big fish. Aluminum sleeves generally have thinner walls and tend to corrode more quickly. Copper sleeves are preferred, whether they are plain or coated with zinc, nickel, or black oxide. Find the sleeve with the smallest inside diameter that fits the wire, cable, or mono you intend to use.

Crimping tools come in two basic styles: point opposing cup (for use with round sleeves) and cup opposing cup (for single- and double-barreled sleeves). It's extremely difficult to achieve a satisfactory crimp with a point-opposing-cup tool. That's why barreled sleeves are superior. For lighter wire, hand tools work well, but if you work with heavy cable, you'll need a swager (a compound tool that gives a mechanical advantage).

The shorter, curved sides of an oval sleeve fit in opposing cups. Be sure to use the smallest cups that fit the sleeve and exert maximum pressure on the crimping tool. Crimps should not be made on the edges of a sleeve, because they will fray the leader. If a sleeve is long enough, you can make a double crimp, taking care to make sure the edges flare and are not crushed.

Crimping Braided Wire

A single sleeve makes it easy to attach braided multi-strand wire to a hook, lure, swivel, or simply to form a loop.

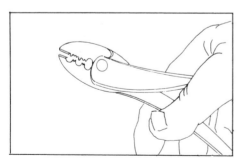

STEP 1 A special crimping tool should be used. Remember that point opposing cup works with round sleeves and cup opposing cup is the choice for oval sleeves.

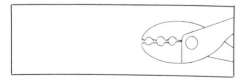

Cup opposing cup crimping tool.

STEP 2 Select the sleeve with the smallest inside diameter that fits the wire. With braided wire, you can use a round single-barrel oval or double-barrel oval. Insert the tag end of the wire through the sleeve and then through the eye of the hook (or form a free-standing loop).

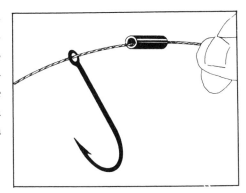

STEP 3 Push the tag end of the wire back through the sleeve, adjusting the size of the loop by positioning the sleeve.

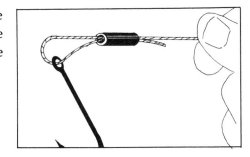

STEP 4 Select the cup in the crimping tool that most closely matches the circumference of the sleeve. Remember that with an oval sleeve, the shorter, curved sides go in the cups. With the loop adjusted to the correct size, position the sleeve in the cup so that the crimp will not crush the edges. Squeeze the tool as hard as you can.

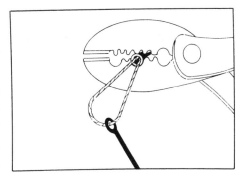

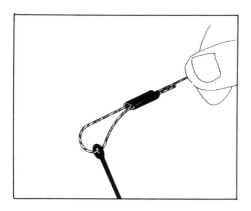

STEP 5 If the sleeve is long enough, you can make two crimps. The first one should be at the end of the sleeve **away** from the hook.

Big-Game Cable Loop

Forty-nine-strand cable is often used for marlin, oversized sharks, and other large denizens of salt water. The connection must withstand a great deal of stress. To add strength to a crimp, loop the cable first and then use two sleeves. Here's how it is done.

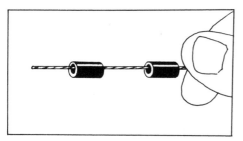

STEP 1 Slip the tag end of the cable through two sleeves of the proper inside diameter.

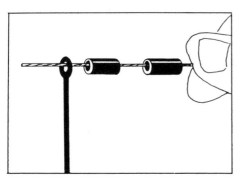

STEP 2 Pass the tag end of the cable through the eye of the hook.

STEP 3 Pass the tag end of the cable through the eye of the hook a second time, leaving about twelve inches of the tag line.

STEP 4 Reduce the size of the loop and hold it in one hand so that it doesn't slip or enlarge. Push the tag end of the cable through the loop to form an Overhand Knot.

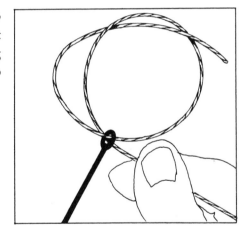

STEP 5 Pass the tag end of the cable through the loop twice more. That's the equivalent of forming a triple Overhand Knot.

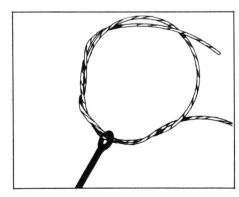

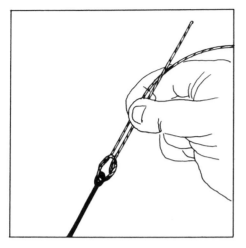

STEP 6 Hold the tag end of the cable alongside and parallel to the standing part. Work the loop down toward the hook eye, pulling on the standing part to form the final size. The loop should be about as tight as you can make it.

STEP 7 Slide the first sleeve over both the tag end and standing part of the cable, working it up as close to the loop as possible.

STEP 8 Crimp the sleeve.

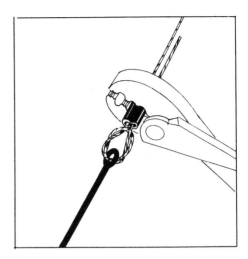

STEP 9 Slide the second sleeve over the tag end. The sleeves should be about one inch apart in actual practice.

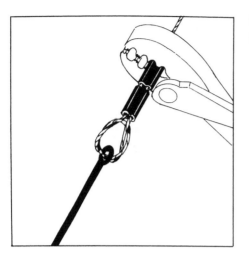

STEP 10 Crimp the second sleeve and trim off any excess of the tag end.

STEP 11 Experts often position the second sleeve so that the tag end is flush with the trailing edge, thus eliminating the need to trim it.

STEP 12 A swivel can be attached the same as a hook.

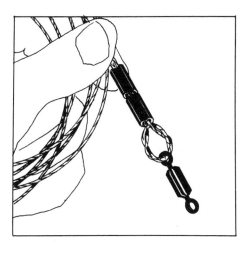

Looping Heavy Mono Leaders

Many offshore and inshore anglers have been using sleeves instead of knots to form loops in heavier monofilament (monofilament from 60 to 200 pounds in strength). This often makes a smaller connection, and if performed correctly is as strong as any knot. It is important to use the size sleeve recommended for the diameter of the monofilament to be joined.

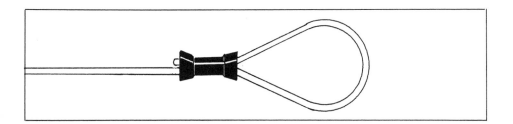

You cannot use the same type crimping pliers that are used to crimp braided wire. Such pliers mash the ends of the sleeves and frequently leave sharp edges that will cut the monofilament.

Instead, a special tool designed for joining monofilament is needed. It is called an opposing cup crimping tool. Such a tool either does not reform the ends of the sleeves when crimped, or it causes the ends of the sleeves, when crimped, to form a shape similar to the mouth of a bugle. This shape will not cut into the monofilament. These tools are available from numerous offshore fishing tackle shops.

Crimping sleeves designed for use with braided wire are NOT recommended for joining monofilament. Use **only crimping sleeves that are especially designed for monofilament**. The Australian offshore fishermen were among the first expert anglers that employed crimping sleeves and monofilament to form loops. They firmly believe that aluminum sleeves are superior to sleeves made from any other material when joining monofilament.

6

Fly-Fishing Knots

○

The heart of any knot system for fly fishing starts with the connection between the fly line and the butt section of the leader. One has several options, but the Nail Knot ranks as the most popular method. Joe Brooks, a noted fly fisherman of the 1950s, learned the knot in Argentina using a horseshoe nail, and brought the technique to the United States. We believe that's how it got its name.

The Nail Knot is actually another application of the snell, which dates back countless centuries. The finished tie is the same, but developing it sometimes takes a different path. Let us show you some variations.

Tube Nail Knot

If you substitute a hollow tube for the traditional nail, you have already improved on the original method.

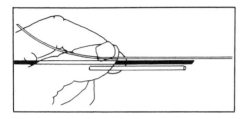

STEP 1 Start with a short hollow tube and lay the fly line against it with the tag end to the right and the standing part to the left. Then, place the butt section of the leader against the tube with its tag end to the left and standing part to the right. Allow about twelve inches of the leader's tag end to form the Nail Knot.

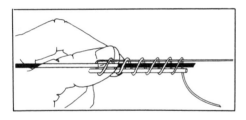

STEP 2 Hold the fly line and leader tightly against the tube with your left hand. Take the tag end of the leader in your right hand and wrap it around the tube, fly line, and standing part of the leader. Notice that the first wrap reverses direction, so that you are working from left to right. In the illustration, we have separated each wrap so you can see the procedure. When you tie the knot, lay each wrap against the one preceding it. Use the fingers of your left hand to keep the wraps from unraveling.

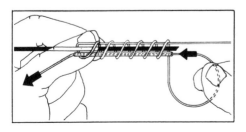

STEP 3 After you have made from six to eight wraps, insert the tag end of the leader through the hollow tube, pushing it from right to left.

STEP 4 Switch hands so that the tube and the wraps are now in your right hand. Be particularly careful to hold the wraps so that they don't unravel. With your left hand, pull the tag end through the tube. Then, remove the tube by sliding it to the left. Don't forget to increase the pressure on the .wraps with the fingers of your right hand so that the wraps don't unwind.

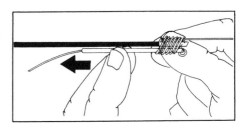

STEP 5 Pull gently on the tag end of the leader until the wraps begin to seat around the fly line. Very carefully, slide the wraps toward the tag end of the fly line, positioning the Nail Knot. Pull on the standing part and tag end of the leader simultaneously to seat the knot firmly.

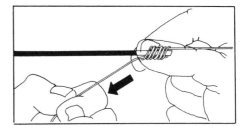

STEP 6 Trim the tag end of the monofilament, and the knot is completed. For added strength, coat it with a rubber-based cement.

Emergency Nail Knot

If you don't have a tube, you can substitute a piece of stiff monofilament doubled over to form a loop. It helps in making the wraps if you have a friend pull gently on the leader as you tie. The knot is fashioned exactly like the Tube Nail Knot with the exception that a loop of monofilament is used to draw the tag end of the leader under the wraps.

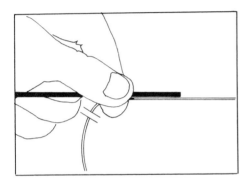

STEP 1 Hold the fly line in your left hand with the tag end facing to the right. Lay the butt section of the leader on top of the fly line with its tag end facing left. Leave about twelve inches of the leader's tag end to tie the knot.

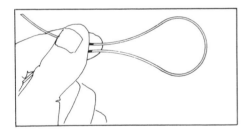

STEP 2 Double a short length of stiff monofilament to form a loop.

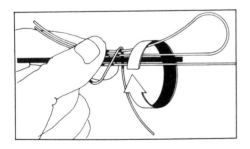

STEP 3 Lay the loop from **Step 2** on the fly line and butt section of the leader, holding all three parts securely with your left hand. Note that the loop faces to the left. Have someone pull gently on the leader to make tying easier. With your right hand, start wrapping the tag end of the leader around the fly line and both

legs of the stiff mono loop, working from left to right.

STEP 4 Take six to eight wraps with the tag end of the leader around the fly line and legs of the mono loop. Then, slip the tag end of the leader through the loop. We have exaggerated the spacing of the wraps for clarity. They should rest tightly against one another. Remember to hold all strands securely in your left hand.

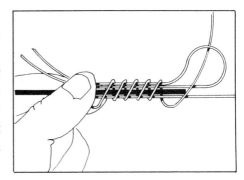

STEP 5 Switch hands, holding the wraps and all the strands in your right hand. With your left hand, pull the two legs of the stiff mono simultaneously, drawing the tag end of the leader under the wraps. It will exit on the left side of the knot.

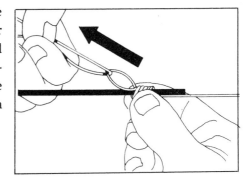

STEP 6 To seat the knot, pull slowly on the tag end of the leader until the wraps begin to tighten. Carefully position the Nail Knot close to the tag end of the fly line. Now pull on the tag end and standing part of the leader at the same time. When the Nail Knot tightens securely, trim the tag end. For added strength and protection, coat the Nail Knot with rubber-based cement.

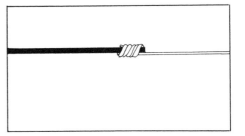

Speedy Nail Knot

The Speedy Nail Knot ranks as the fastest and easiest method for attaching a tapered leader or the butt section of a leader to the fly line. It will not work when the sections of a leader are knotted together. The tying technique parallels that for snelling a hook. If you can snell a hook, you can tie the Speedy Nail Knot. The needle merely acts as a stiffener to support the fly line and leader. The smaller the diameter of the needle, the less slack encountered when the needle is removed and the knot seated.

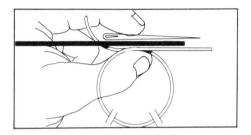

STEP 1 Hold the fly line in your left hand with the standing part to the left and the tag end to the right. Place a small needle on the fly line with the point of the needle to the right. Then, lay the tag end of the leader on the needle so that the end extends about one inch beyond the point of the needle.

Bring the other tag end of the leader (this is the tag end of the leader to which a fly will be attached or the remainder of the leader built) around to form a big loop under the needle. About two or three inches of this tag end extends to the left after the loop is made. Hold everything together securely with the left hand.

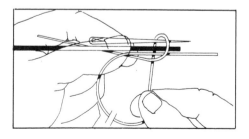

STEP 2 Take the right leg of the loop in your right hand and start wrapping it around the fly line, leader, and needle. The wraps will move from right to left.

STEP 3 Continue the wraps in **Step 2** until you have six to eight wraps. It is essential that you hold everything securely with your left hand and keep the leg of the loop in your right hand taut. Any slack will cause the wraps to unravel. Note that each wrap is laid tightly against the preceding one.

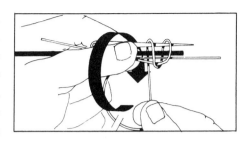

STEP 4 When you have completed the required number of wraps, use the fingers of your left hand to hold them in place. With your right hand, pull slowly and steadily on the tag end of the leader; you started with about one inch extending specifically for this purpose. Keep pulling until you have drawn the entire leader under the wraps.

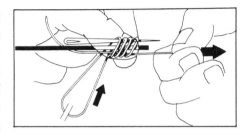

STEP 5 Pull on the tag end and the standing part of the leader simultaneously to semi-tighten the Nail Knot over the needle. Then, carefully work the needle loose from under the wraps and remove it. Remember that the needle slides out from right to left.

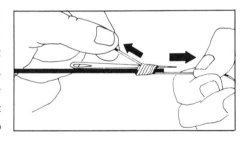

STEP 6 Position the Nail Knot on the fly line and tighten it completely by pulling on the tag end and standing part at the same time. Trim the tag end and the Speedy Nail Knot is finished. With practice, you should be able to tie this in less than fifteen seconds.

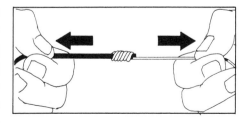

Double Nail-Knot Loop

One of the fastest methods for putting a loop in the end of a fly line, the Double Nail Knot Loop can be tied in the field using a needle, paper clip, or similar stiffener. It consists of nothing more than two Speedy Nail Knots tied in series. For best results, use twelve to fifteen-pound-test monofilament and **don't** strip the finish from the fly line. This will allow the mono to dig into the coating.

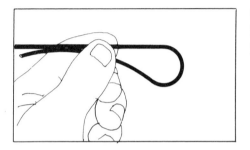

STEP 1 Fold the tag end of the fly line back on itself, creating a loop and leaving a tag end of about two inches.

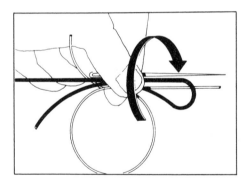

STEP 2 Place a needle, paper clip, or tube on the fly line as a stiffener. Use an eighteen- to twenty-four-inch length of monofilament testing twelve pounds to fifteen pounds. Loop it beneath the stiffener with about one inch extending on either end. Continue just as you would if you were tying the Speedy Nail Knot (see instructions).

STEP 3 Tighten the first Speedy Nail Knot and trim both tag ends.

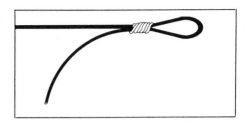

STEP 4 Build a second Speedy Nail Knot right behind the first. Draw it tight and trim the tag ends.

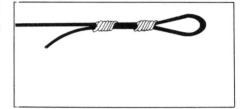

STEP 5 Trim the tag end of the fly line. For added strength, coat both Nail Knots with a rubber-based cement.

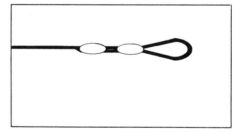

Needle Nail Knot

The Needle Nail Knot makes an extremely strong and smooth connection between the fly line and the butt section of the leader. It will not hang up in the rod guides, nor will it snag debris as it is moved through the water.

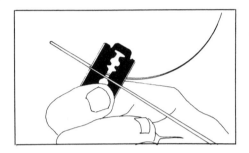

STEP 1 Using a double-edge razor blade (single-edge blades are rarely sharp enough), grip the leader in your left hand about three inches from the tag end. Make sure the natural curl of the monofilament faces toward you. Hold the razor blade at a right angle to the monofilament and gently push the blade forward. The blade will bite into the mono and slice a portion of it. With a little practice, this slicing motion becomes routine. Repeat the slicing operation several times until you have shaved the monofilament into a very thin, pointed end that will pass through the eye of a small needle.

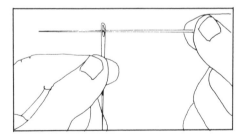

STEP 2 Select a very small needle and insert two to three inches of the shaved monofilament through the eye.

STEP 3 The drawing shows the threaded needle being inserted into the fly line using a pair of pliers to force it through. A better procedure is to insert the needle into the fly line and out the side (about ¼ to ⁵⁄₁₆ inch from the tag end) before you thread the eye with the mono.

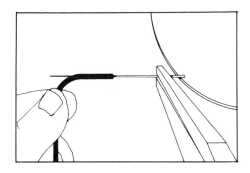

STEP 4 With the thumb and forefinger of one hand, firmly hold the fly line with the needle inside it. Use pliers to grasp the pointed end of the needle and pull it all the way through the section of fly line. As the needle exits the fly line, the mono threaded through the eye will follow easily.

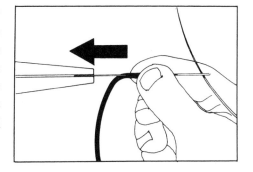

STEP 5 Lay the needle aside temporarily. Pull the shaved end of the leader until about six inches extends beyond the exit point in the fly line.

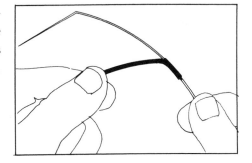

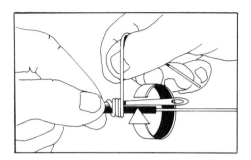

STEP 6 Place the needle on top of the fly line with the eye to the right and the point facing left. With the tag end of the leader, make three to five wraps around the needle and the fly line. Use the fingers of your left hand to hold the wraps in place.

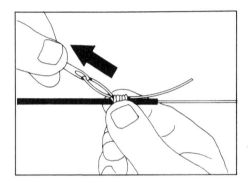

STEP 7 Insert the shaved end of the mono through the eye of the needle again. With pliers, pull the needle to the left, drawing it under the wraps and out.

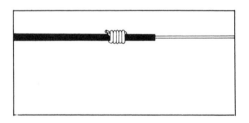

STEP 8 Hold the standing part of the leader in one hand and the tag end in the other. Pull both strands together until the knot tightens around the fly line. Trim the tag end, and the knot is completed.

Needle Nail Knot—Mono Loop

To make a very fine monofilament loop in the back end of a shooting head or a loop at the front of a fly line, consider this knot. With smaller lines for dry-fly fishing, you can use mono as light as twelve-pound test; for tougher assignments, increase the breaking strength of the mono accordingly. A fly-tying vise or similar tool makes construction easier.

STEP 1 Insert a very small needle through the tag end of the fly line for a distance of about one-half inch, and force the needle point through the coating of the fly line as shown. Put the point of the needle in a vise. Shave both ends of a twelve-inch length of monofilament of the appropriate breaking strength and insert both ends through the eye of the needle. Grip the fly line between the tag end and the spot where the needle exits. Pull the fly line over the eye of the needle until both ends of the monofilament exit the fly line.

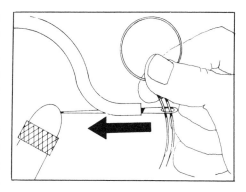

STEP 2 Pull both ends of the monofilament until a loop of the desired size is formed in front of the tag end of the fly line. Lay the needle alongside the fly line with the eye of the needle to the right. Make three to five wraps around the needle and fly line with both ends of the monofilament. Each wrap should seat tightly against the preceding one.

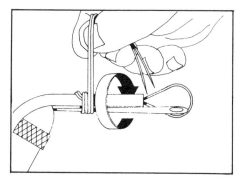

STEP 3 Hold the wraps with the fingers of your left hand so that they don't unravel and thread both shaved ends of the monofilament through the eye of the needle.

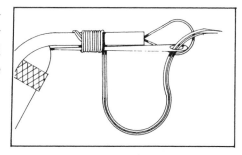

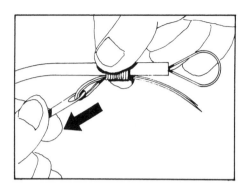

STEP 4 Pull the needle and shaved ends under the coils so that they exit to the left. Be sure to keep holding the wraps in place.

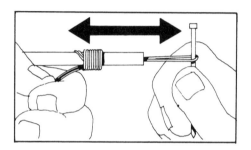

STEP 5 To tighten, insert a nail or some other object through the loop. Grip the tag ends of the mono in your other hand and pull until the knot tightens completely.

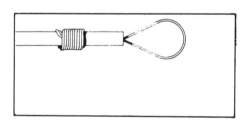

STEP 6 Use nail clippers to trim the tag ends as close to the wraps as possible.

Paragum Knot

Fly fishermen challenged with the task of catching very large trout on tiny flies with gossamer tippets have developed a special shock-absorbing leader. The same idea can be used with other types of tackle.

Paragum or Shock Gum (made in Europe and sold in a number of fly shops) comes in small coils. It looks like monofilament, but boasts some of the characteristics of a rubber band. You can stretch a piece in your hand.

This special knot replaces the typical monofilament knots that tend to fail with this material. Paragum is usually tied into a tapered leader between the tippet and the next larger section—though it can be even more effective between two sections of a braided leader.

STEP 1 The Paragum Knot is actually a pair of Uni-Knots tied back to back. The Paragum in the drawing is on the right and appears hatched. The mono leader tippet (on the left) looks clear. Hold the leader tippet from left to right, leaving about six inches of tag end to tie the knot. The Paragum is held from right to left with six inches of tag end extending past the junction. Loop the tag end of the leader back to the left and make five wraps around the tippet and the Paragum.

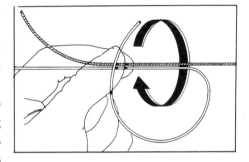

STEP 2 Use the fingers of your left hand to keep the wraps from uncoiling. Pull slowly on the tag end until the loop disappears. Try to make each wrap close to the one before. This aids in seating the knot.

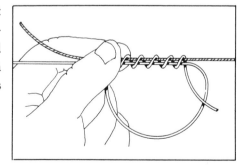

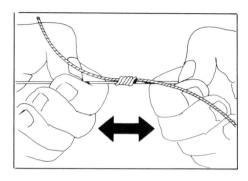

STEP 3 Pull simultaneously on the tag end and standing part of the leader tippet to tighten the knot partially.

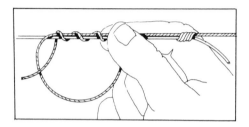

STEP 4 Follow the same procedure with the Paragum, forming a second knot identical to the first.

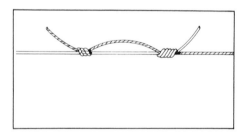

STEP 5 At the completion of **Step 4,** the knots should look like this.

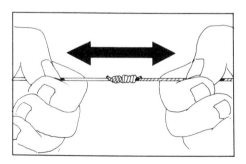

STEP 6 Pull on the standing part of the tippet and the standing part of the Paragum to draw the knots together. They will seat against each other, forming a strong connection. Trim the tag ends.

A conventional Surgeon's Knot serves well for attaching Paragum to braided leader material.

Whip-Finishing a Fly or Jig

The Whip-Finish gets our vote as the best technique for securing the thread after dressing a fly or jig. Although you'll find several variations, we like this one because it can be completed in seconds. It also enables the tyer to secure the thread at any position along the hook shank.

STEP 1 After the final wrap has been made, pull about eight inches of thread from the bobbin. Place the forefinger and middle finger of your right hand **under** the thread as shown.

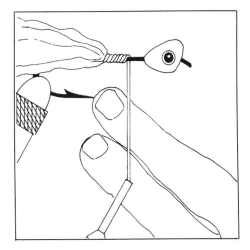

STEP 2 Maintain light tension against the thread with the two fingers. Rotate your fingers slightly upward and in a half circle to the right to form a loop in the thread.

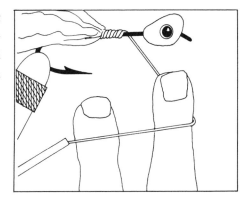

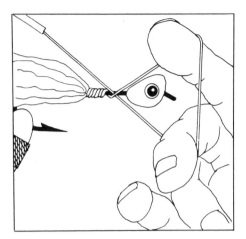

STEP 3 By rotating the two fingers, the thread is wrapped around the hook shank. With each revolution, the forefinger passes **over** the hook shank, while the middle finger pulls down and creates tension on the thread. **Note that the middle finger does not pass over the hook.**

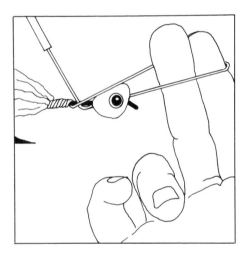

STEPS 4 THROUGH 7 Continue rotating the two fingers inside the loop of thread, laying wrap after wrap around the hook shank.

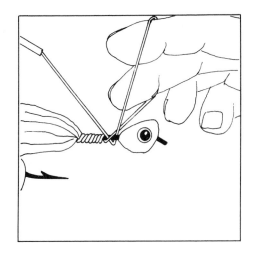

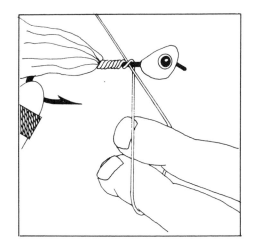

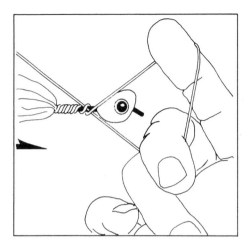

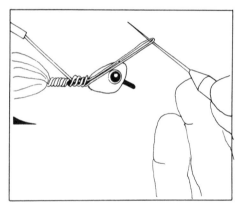

STEP 8 When a satisfactory number of wraps have been made, slip a needle, scissor points, or any smooth object into the loop. Pull on the bobbin or the thread with your left hand to seat the Whip-Finish. Cut the thread and coat with head cement.

Whipping a Loop in Fly Line

A loop in the forward end of the fly line allows an angler to change leaders easily, while one at the other end facilitates attaching backing. To insure maximum strength, don't strip the outer covering from the fly line so the thread can dig into it. That is accomplished by swinging the bobbin rapidly under pressure. The faster it swings, the greater the effect of centrifugal force and the tighter the wraps.

STEP 1 Use a fly-tying bobbin with size-A thread (Nymo, flat waxed, Kevlar, or any quality thread). Insert the thread through the tube of the bobbin as you normally would. Then, remove the spool and wrap the thread around one of the bobbin legs **four** times before reseating the spool. The four turns will give you the tension necessary to swing the bobbin with force. If you need more thread, you will have to rotate the spool with your hands to feed the additional amount. To start, fold the fly line back on itself for about two inches to form a loop.

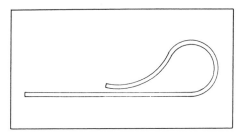

STEP 2 Lay the tag end of the thread parallel to the tag end of the fly line and make a few turns by hand to secure the loop. Grip the loop in your right hand and the fly line (both standing part and tag end) in your left hand. Rotate your hands away from your body to swing the bobbin. The faster you spin it, the deeper the thread will bury in the outer coating of the fly line. With practice, you can lay each wrap against the preceding one.

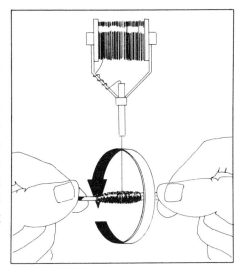

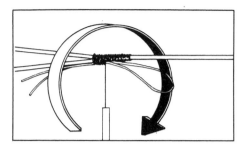

STEP 3 A wrap of ½ inch is adequate, but you might want to stretch it to ⅝ or ¾ of an inch. Stop before you reach that distance, and taper the tag end of the fly line with a sharp knife or razor. This will help to make a smooth transition as you wrap over it down to the single strand of fly line. To secure the wraps so they don't unravel, use a Whip-Finish (instructions above). Many anglers prefer to lay a ten-inch piece of doubled mono with the loop in the direction the wraps are going. Mono testing four to ten pounds is adequate. Make eight or ten wraps by swinging the bobbin gently. If you swing it too hard, you won't be able to pull the mono back out.

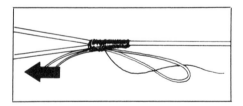

STEP 4 Cut the thread coming from the bobbin and slip the tag end through the loop of monofilament. Hold the fly line and pull both tag ends of the monofilament at the same time. This will draw the thread under the wraps and secure it.

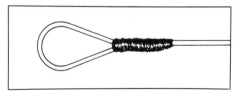

STEP 5 Trim the thread at the point where it exits the wraps. Then coat the wraps with a glue or rubber-based cement such as Pliobond. **Take a moment to test the loop.** Place a smooth object in the loop and pull on it with

one hand while holding the fly line in the other. If the thread did not bury deeply enough, the loop will pull out.

Improved Turle Knot

The Turle Knot has been a popular tie for connecting a fly with a turned-up or turned-down eye to the leader tippet. It does not work well with ring-eye hooks.

STEP 1 Insert the tag end of the tippet through the hook eye. Leave several inches of tag end for tying this knot. Bring the tag end around and over itself to form a loop as shown.

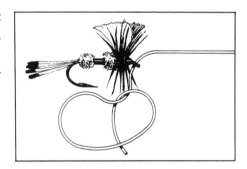

STEP 2 Pass the tag end twice through the loop created in **Step 1** (refer to illustration). This creates a Double Overhand Knot.

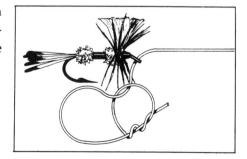

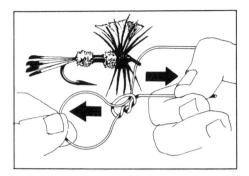

STEP 3 Hold the loop in one hand and the tag end in the other. Pull on the tag end firmly to seat the Double Overhand Knot.

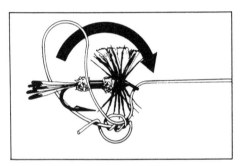

STEP 4 Drop the tag end through the remaining loop (this will increase the knot's strength) and pull the loop open so that it will slip over the fly. Pass the loop over the fly.

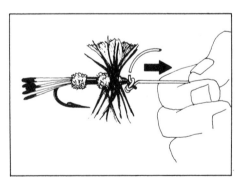

STEP 5 Pull slowly on the leader as you tease the knot into position around the hook eye. Continue pulling until the knot tightens. Trim the tag end.

STEP 6 The finished knot offers a straight pull and will not cant when presented to a fish.

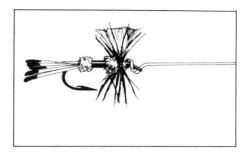

George Harvey Dry Fly Knot

We have not found a better knot for attaching a dry fly (or any fly with a turned-up or turned-down eye) to a leader tippet. It was developed by George Harvey, the pioneer instructor of fly tying and fly fishing at Penn State University. Tied properly, this knot rarely breaks. It merely involves two procedures performed twice.

STEP 1 Insert about four to six inches of tippet through the front of the hook eye as shown. If you push the tippet through the back of the hook eye, the fly will ride unnaturally.

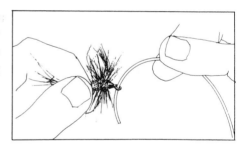

STEP 2 This is one of the few knots where you don't hold the fly or the hook at this stage. Instead, hold the tag end and standing part of the tippet together. Using the tag end, make a circle around the standing part about the size of a dime or smaller. A larger circle makes it difficult to finish the knot.

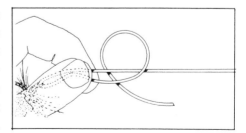

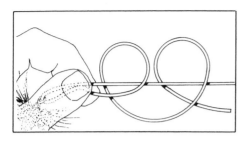

STEP 3 Make a second circle of the same size around the standing part.

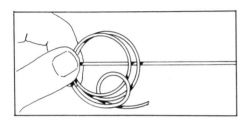

STEP 4 Hold the two circles together and pass the tag end of the tippet through both circles.

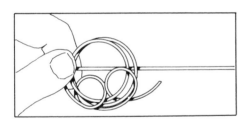

STEP 5 Make a second pass with the tag end through both circles. Be sure to continue holding the circles in your left hand.

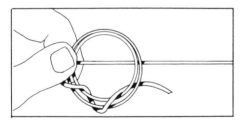

STEP 6 At this stage, the knot should look like the illustration.

STEP 7 Now hold the fly by the bend of the hook in your left hand. Pull on the standing part of the tippet. **If the knot is tied correctly, the two circles will slide back and jump up and over the hook eye.** If they don't, the knot is tied incorrectly.

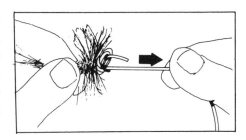

STEP 8 Continue pulling on the standing part of the tippet while holding the fly until the knot fully tightens. The knot involves two circles around the standing part and two passes with the tag end through the circles. That's it.

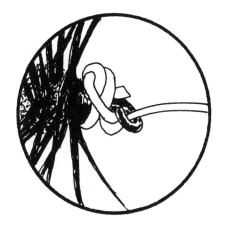

Dropper Loop

Fly fishermen often want to fish more than one nymph or wet fly at the same time. Additional flies are known as droppers and a loop is an excellent way to attach them. Those who fish for bait with conventional or spinning gear often use several small jigs or quills. Again, the Dropper Loop provides the answer. It can either be used as a loop, or one leg of the loop can be cut at the spot where it meets the standing part of the line to form a longer, single strand. Here's how that loop is made.

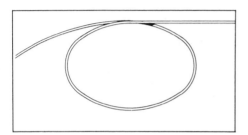

STEP 1 Make a circle in the line where you want to attach the dropper. The size of the circle determines the size of the loop.

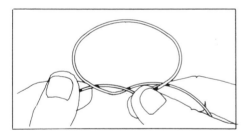

STEP 2 Take the top strand of the circle and wrap it around itself three or four times.

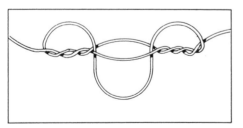

STEP 3 Reach down and pull the bottom leg of the circle through the center of the wraps created in **Step 2**.

STEP 4 This is what the Dropper Loop looks like before tightening.

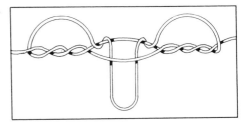

STEP 5 Moisten the wraps. Then, pull sharply at both sides of the standing part at the same time. Don't pull on the loop. It will form by itself.

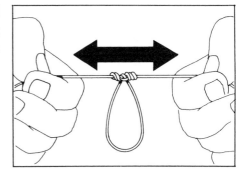

7

Putting it all Together

O

Shock Leader of Monofilament or Wire

Light-tackle fishing has become a way of life along most sections of coastline and countless inland waters. When challenging fish that boast sharp dentures, knife-edge gill plates, or an abrasive body, fine-diameter line seldom survives. A critter with honed teeth can instantly sever heavy monofilament.

Depending on the species, anglers solve the problem by attaching a shock leader of heavier monofilament and add a trace of wire if teeth pose a threat. The same system makes sense in fresh water. The smaller the diameter of the line, the better it casts, and the deeper a lure will run when tethered to that mono. All you have to do to eliminate the risk of having the line fray around the mouth of the fish or on the bottom is tie in a short section of heavier monofilament. An angler fishing with lines testing four to eight pounds may employ a shock leader of twelve- or fifteen-pound test. It's all relative.

Virtually every knot system we use starts with the Bimini Twist. Tied correctly, the Bimini is stronger than the unknotted line and adds vital strength to any combination of knots that follow.

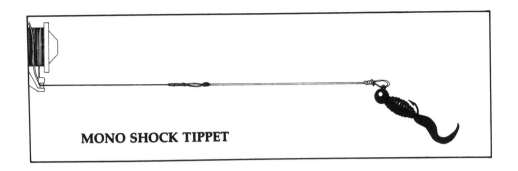

MONO SHOCK TIPPET

DRAWING 1 Before adding a monofilament shock leader, build a Bimini Twist in the tag end of the fishing line. Several knots can be used to attach the heavier monofilament to the Bimini. We recommend the Surgeon's, Albright, or Huffnagle.

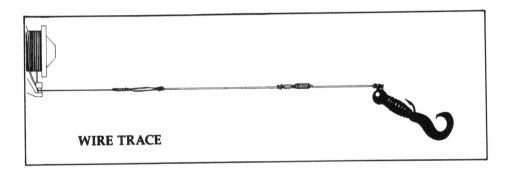

WIRE TRACE

DRAWING 2 In some situations, you will need stronger monofilament to protect against abrasion and a short trace of even heavier mono or wire next to the hook or lure. Start by tying a Bimini Twist in the tag end of the line and attaching the Bimini to the stronger mono with an Albright or Surgeon's Knot. Heavier mono or braided wire can be added with a Huffnagle, Albright, or Surgeon's Knot. If you use single-strand wire, put a Haywire Twist Loop in one end and flatten the loop with pliers. Attach the mono to the wire with an Albright. A Haywire Twist to the hook or lure finishes the rig.

Making a Fish-Finder Rig

Bottom fishermen (particularly those probing the surf) want the fish to pick up the bait and move off before it detects the weight of the sinker. That can be accomplished with the Fish-Finder Rig, in which the sinker

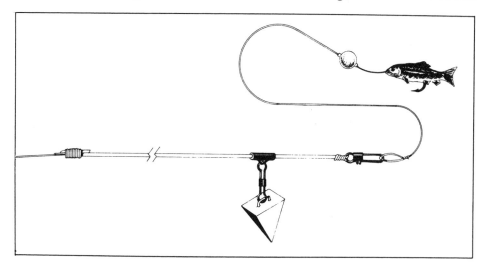

slides on a mono shock leader. Start with a Bimini in the fishing line and connect the shock leader with an Albright, Surgeon's, or Huffnagle Knot. Many tackle shops sell a Fish Finder, which is nothing more than a sleeve and a snap for hanging the sinker.

There are several ways to make your own. A snap swivel works if you pass the line through the top eye of the swivel and hang the sinker from the snap. You can also take a piece of heavy mono and, using sleeves and a crimping tool, connect one end to the sinker and make a loop in the other end. Run the line through the loop and you have a Fish Finder.

Tie a snap at the other end of the shock leader and you can change rigs quickly. If you want the bait to ride a few inches above the bottom, position a small float a short distance in front of the hook. Many of these floats are painted fluorescent colors and help to attract predators.

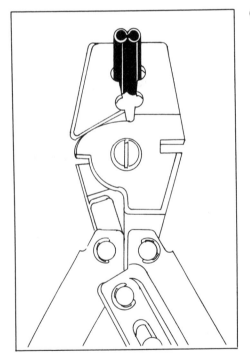

Cup opposing cup crimping tool.

A finished Fish-finding rig.

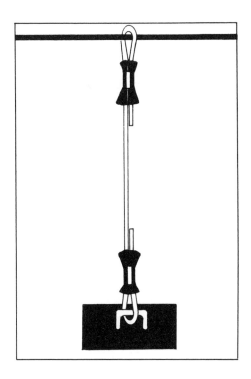

Storing Fly-Fishing Tippets

Most saltwater fly-fishing leader systems center around a class tippet with a Bimini Twist tied in both ends. It takes time to build a pair of Biminis, particularly when you want to achieve a specific distance between them. Veteran anglers often put the Biminis in tippet sections while they watch television at home or whenever they find some extra time.

Storing these tippet sections is easy. Obtain a small line spool or even one originally made to hold 8mm film. Drill two or three pairs of holes in the rim of the spool so you can secure the last tippet without a knot or rubber band. Then, put the tippets on the spool, interlocking adjacent Biminis. Push the last Bimini up through one hole in the spool rim and down through the other. You can carry the spool easily and you're always ready to rig.

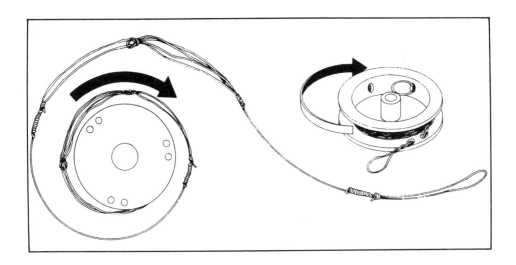

Four Methods for Building Fly Leaders

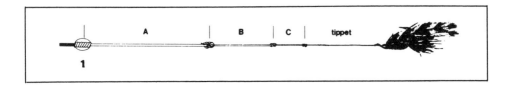

DRAWING 1 An unwarranted mystique shrouds the simplicity of building tapered fly-fishing leaders. If you can tie a Surgeon's Knot, you have the ability to join sections of monofilament of different diameter. Construction of a basic leader with a light tippet for everything from salmon and steelhead to bonefish and permit follows a simple formula.

With the exception of a leader for

dry-fly fishing, you only need a butt section, two intermediate segments, and the tippet. Start by determining how long you want the total leader to be. The butt section will be slightly less than one-half the leader length. With a little practice, you will be able to approximate it with reasonable accuracy. For most assignments, monofilament testing twenty pounds (no more than twenty-five-pound test) works well.

The second leader segment (B in the illustration) is one-half the length of the butt section; and the next segment (C) is one-half of Segment B. For most fishing situations, a two-foot length of monofilament works well as the tippet. The following example should help you put it all together.

Let's assume you want to build a 10½ leader for bonefish, bass, or any other fish. Make the butt section five feet of twenty-five-pound test. Segment B will measure two and a half feet of twenty-pound test. Drop to fifteen-pound test for Segment C and make it fifteen inches long (one-half of two and a half feet). Add two feet of tippet and you have a leader that measures ten feet nine inches.

Remember that to adjust the total length of the leader, you simply change the length of the butt section and all else will fall into place.

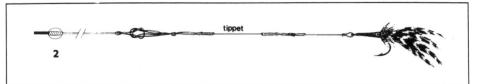

2

DRAWING 2 The basic saltwater fly leader has only three sections: the butt, class tippet, and shock tippet. Breaking strengths, as well as the type of shock tippet may vary, but the construction remains the same.

Attach the butt section of the leader to the fly line with a Nail Knot or a loop. Typically, the butt section tests between twenty-five pounds and forty pounds. Tie a Surgeon's Loop in the other end of the butt section. This loop-to-loop system makes it easy to change flies and leaders because the butt section is semi-permanent.

Put a Bimini Twist in both ends of the light (class) tippet. If you followed our earlier suggestion, you already have a number of these looped together on a small spool. Double one of the Biminis and tie a Surgeon's Knot. Trim the tag end. Then interlock this loop with the loop on the butt section.

The final step lies in attaching the shock leader (heavier mono or wire). We recommend that you use the Bimini Twist in the end of the light tippet to build an Albright, Surgeon's, or Huffnagle Knot. Some anglers carry a number of fly patterns already rigged with the shock tippet and class tippet already tied. Special carrying cases are available for this arrangement. To change flies, you simply unloop the leader where the butt section and class tippet connect, and loop on another.

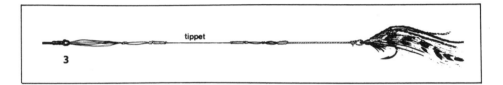

DRAWING 3 When the water is off-color or the fish are not leader shy, you may want to eliminate the butt section of the leader. The shorter the leader, the easier it is to turn the fly over in a wind. Shorter leaders also perform better with sinking lines, causing the fly to swim deeper.

In this example, a light tippet is attached directly to a shock tippet of heavier material. Start by putting a loop in the end of your fly line or using a very short butt section with a loop in the end. Tie a Bimini Twist in both ends of the tippet and make a Surgeon's Loop in one end as outlined for **Drawing 2.** Interlock this loop with the one on your fly line Connect the shock leader with an Al bright, Surgeon's or Huffnagle Knot.

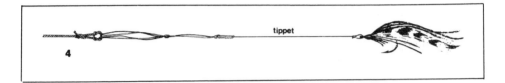

tippet

4

DRAWING 4 When you want to get the fly down quickly in fast water with a sinking line, or you simply want the fly at the same level in the water column as the line, try this type of leader. It works well for Pacific salmon in Alaska, largemouth bass in deeper water, and other species when they're in deep water. When looking at a fly beneath the surface, fish are seldom as leader shy as most people suspect.

This leader is nothing more than two or three feet of tippet tied directly to the fly. Put a Bimini Twist in one end of the tippet and then make the Surgeon's Loop we described above. Interlock that with the loop in the end of your sinking fly line and connect the other end of the tippet to the fly. It may not impress those folks who measure every leader section carefully and make advanced mathematical calculations, but it catches fish. In fact, we have taken trophy rainbow trout in excess of ten pounds on a leader of this design that measured less than six inches.

Using Wire in Fly Leaders

DRAWING 1 With single-strand wire, a Haywire Twist is the standard connection for attaching a fly, bare hook, or anything else. Instructions are detailed elsewhere in the text. Note that in this illustration, the distance between twists is exaggerated for clarity.

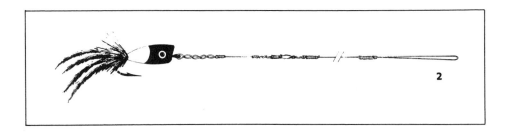

DRAWING 2 If wire is required as a shock tippet in a standard saltwater

fly leader, here's the procedure—
starting with the fly. A Haywire Twist
connects the single-strand wire to the
fly. Put a Haywire Twist Loop in the
back end of the single-strand wire
and flatten the loop. Tie a Bimini
Twist in the tag end of the class tippet
and use an Albright Knot to attach
the monofilament to the wire. A Bimini Twist and a Surgeon's Loop in
the other end of the class tippet allows you to loop it on the butt section.

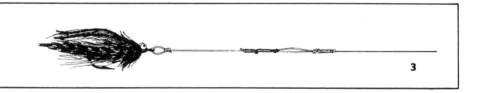

DRAWING 3 When braided wire is
used (coated or uncoated), an Albright Knot connects it to the class
tippet. Be sure to tie a Bimini Twist in
the class tippet prior to building the
Albright. At times, you may want the
fly to swing freely rather than be tethered tightly to the leader. With
braided wire, a Homer Rhode or Non-
Slip Mono Loop does the job.

DRAWINGS 4A AND 4B The Figure-8 Knot (described elsewhere in the text) is the simplest and quickest way to tie braided wire to a fly. Remember that if you leave a tag end slightly longer than you would with monofilament, you can untie the knot and change flies without shortening the shock tippet.

Dry-Fly Leader

Many experts think that the most critical factor in getting a stubborn trout to take a dry fly centers on a drag-free float in a natural manner, rather than on the pattern selected. Even the most apt pattern will not take fish if poorly presented.

Leader construction plays an important role in presentation. Certain practitioners guard secret formulas for building their own tapered leaders. You can follow this cult if you choose, but we recommend using commercially made, tapered leaders with a slight modification.

Experience shows that medium-soft material in the butt section assists in achieving a better turn-over. Not every caster knows why braided leaders seem to work well. The answer lies in the softness of the butt section.

When the rod is stopped at the end of the forward cast, the line begins to unroll from the rod tip toward the target. As the unrolling fly line reaches the leader, a softer butt section transmits the unrolling more precisely than a stiffer butt. Stiffness causes a leader to stand up rather than unroll. Most leaders available commercially have the medium-soft butt necessary for good turn-over.

With a commercially made, knotted, tapered leader, we recommend you eliminate the last section and tie a Non-Slip Mono Loop or Surgeon's Loop in the tag end of the next-to-last segment. If the leader is knotless, fold back the last two feet of tippet and tie a loop. Trim off the tag end.

From your fly vest, take a length of 5X tippet material and tie an identical loop in one end. Interlock the two loops and you can change tippets easily. When you have cut back the tippet, simply replace it with a new, looped section. For example, a popular eastern U.S. dry-fly leader is nine feet long, tapered to a 5X. If you remove the last two feet

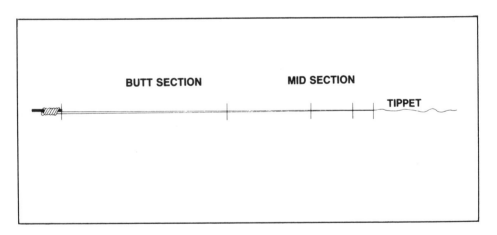

and make a loop, you then have a seven-foot leader. Add your own tippet and you have a top-quality nine-foot leader plus the ability to change tippets quickly. Now, refer to **Drawing 1**. It illustrates the essentials of presentation and leader construction.

DRAWINGS 1A, 1B, 1C We already know that the key to success hinges on a drag-free float. Even if it does drift drag-free, you must be able to cast the fly accurately to reach the fish. These two factors are determined primarily by the tippet's length and diameter. A 5X tippet generally performs effectively—though, obviously, tippet strength must be increased for bigger fish.

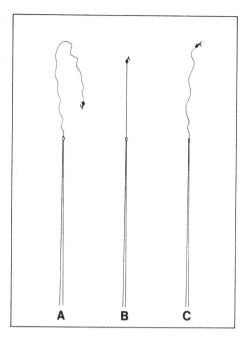

Any leader that falls straight on the water will almost surely be affected by drag. To benefit from a drag-free float, you must have a certain amount of slack in the tippet just before the fly. While formulas have been advanced for matching the tippet size to the hook size, we feel these are invalid. You can dress several different types of dry flies on one hook size (such as Catskill tie, hair wing, and spider), and each of the three will offer a different amount of air resistance. To determine the correct tippet and length, you must actually cast the fly when it is attached to the tippet. Then, after observing how the fly and leader fall to the water, you make the necessary adjustments.

In **Drawing 1A,** the tippet has fallen back on itself. Plenty of slack exists in front of the fly, so a drag-free float should occur. In the trade-off, accuracy suffers. **Drawing 1B** shows that the leader has been shortened and the fly reattached. Now the leader and tippet falls straight. This means the tippet is either too short or too heavy. Without slack in the tippet, drag will occur quickly.

Drawing 1C illustrates how a properly built dry-fly leader should appear on the water's surface at the end of the cast. Remember that if the leader falls back on itself, the tippet is too long or too thin. If it falls straight, the tippet is too short or too heavy. By adjusting **only** the tippet on a well-designed tapered leader, you can increase your success fishing dry flies.

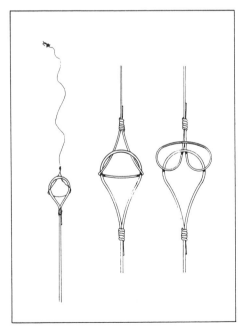

DRAWING 2 Most people build or buy tapered leaders and sacrifice tippet material every time they knot a new tippet to the taper. Just tying the knot sacrifices a portion of the leader. After several tippets have been attached, the original taper has been destroyed.

For years we have recommended another system that is surprisingly strong and extremely effective. It's the loop-to-loop method described above. Simply fold back two feet of the tippet and put a loop in the leader. You can then loop on as many new tippets as necessary without ever changing the taper. When you do make the loop-to-loop connection, make sure that the two loops form a Square Knot rather than a Girth Hitch. The Girth Hitch (far right) is a cutting connection, but the Square Knot distributes the load evenly and doesn't break.

8

Some Final Thoughts

○

Learning to tie knots well focuses on a state of mind rather than physical ability or lack of it. For someone who has never seen it done, tying a shoelace stands out as a major challenge. Most of us could do it blindfolded without sacrificing speed. Those of us who tie the Bimini Twist regularly handle it as comfortably as putting on a pair of shoes. Any knot can be mastered on a step-by-step basis once you make up your mind you can do it.

We don't suggest that you become proficient with every knot in this book, but rather with the handful that will serve your daily needs. To tie them effectively, you must practice periodically or fish enough so that you continue tying them. Keep this volume as reference and you can always go back to it when necessary. And, if you have resisted learning the Bimini Twist because you deem it too complicated, please reconsider. It is by far the most important knot in this book and the basis for the majority of leader systems.

Since you already know how to tie your shoes, we thought we would leave you with a variation that keeps the laces from coming untied easily. Then, let us show you a way to tie your boat with a strong hitch that does release instantly. It's a handy knot to know.

Non-Slip Shoelace Knot

Aboard a boat or in the field, this method for tying your shoes prevents the laces from loosening. If you have young children, you may want to teach it to them.

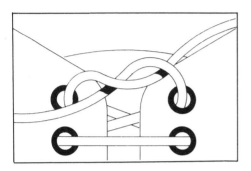

STEP 1 Cross one lace over the other and snug it up just as if you were tying your shoes the standard way.

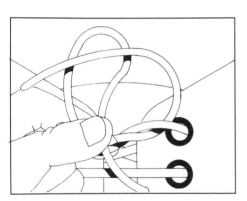

STEP 2 Double back a tag end to form one loop of a bow and pass the other tag end in front of this loop.

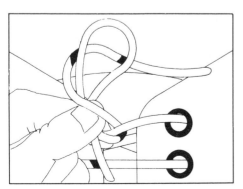

STEP 3 Continue passing the tag end around the loop and behind it.

STEP 4 Take another complete turn with the tag end around the loop. Then bend the lace near the tag end to double it and push the doubled end through the center of the two turns, forming the other side of the bow.

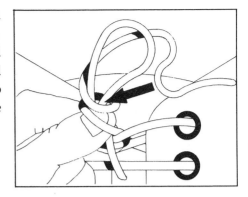

STEP 5 Tighten the bow by pulling on both loops. With some laces, you may have to tease them a little bit to make the bow uniform.

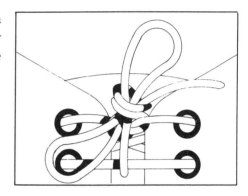

STEP 6 The finished knot looks like this and will not loosen easily by it-self.

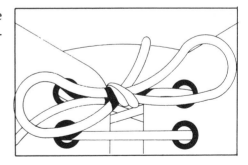

Quick-Release Knot

There are a number of ways to tie the Quick-Release Knot. This is one of them.

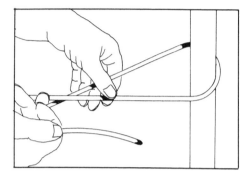

STEP 1 Pass the tag end of the line around a post or other object and under the standing part. Leave about two feet to complete the knot.

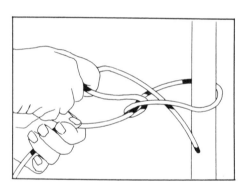

STEP 2 Reach through the loop created in **Step 1** and pull the tag line through **partially,** forming a second loop. Be sure that the very end of the tag line does not get pulled through.

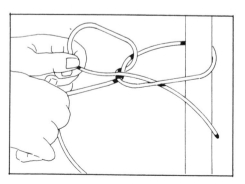

STEP 3 Pull gently on the standing part to close the main loop partially.

STEP 4 Reach through the second loop created in **Step 2** and grip the tag end in its center, pulling it partially through the loop.

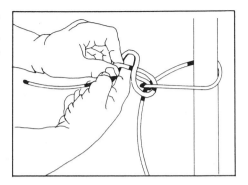

STEP 5 Pull the standing part of the line to tighten the Quick-Release Knot. You can put maximum pressure on the standing part and the knot will hold. Tug on the tag end and the knot comes apart instantly.

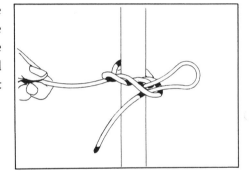

Index of Knots

○

Personal Knot Notes

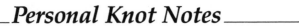

Personal Knot Notes

Personal Knot Notes